IMAGES OF
MULLINGAR

IMAGES OF
MULLINGAR

Ruth Illingworth

N
NONSUCH

First published 2008

Nonsuch Publishing
73 Lower Leeson Street
Dublin 2
Ireland
www.nonsuchireland.com

British Library Cataloguing in Publication Data.
A catalogue record for this book is available from the British Library.

ISBN 978 1 84588 925 8

Typesetting and origination by Nonsuch Publishing
Printed and bound in Great Britain by Athenaeum Press Ltd.

Contents

Acknowledgements

I wish to express my particular gratitude to Davy Hynes, who gave so much of his time to scan photographs for me. I also want to thank Mrs Ber Hynes for her wonderful hospitality.

Grateful thanks to the staff of Westmeath County Library for all their help in supplying photographs, and other material, from the Library collection.

I also wish to express my gratitude to Philip Tierney, for his permission to use material from his collection of photographs and postcards (The Tierney Collection); Leo and Bill Daly for permission to use their photographs (The Daly Collection); Eilis Ryan, Editor, *Westmeath Examiner* for permission to use photos from the *Examiner* collections; Danny Dunne for help with scanning photographs; Fr Joseph Gallagher, Mullingar Cathedral, for permission to use material from the Cathedral Museum; Sean Magee, for scanning photographs, and permission to use material from his collections, and Sister Assumpta Guinan, for permission to use materials from the Presentation Convent Archives.

I would also like to express my deepest thanks to all those who donated photographs for use in this book: Johnny McGregor, Jim Doherty, Paddy Begley, Paddy Colgan, Brian Fagan, Noel Cox, Rita Tynan, Eddie Reilly, Anthony Hughes, Geraldine Flynn, Robert Heath, John McCauley, Olive Winckworth, Betty Tynan, Sinead Gilligan, Mrs D. Brock and Aodhan Moynihan.

A special word of thanks to Joe and Frances Gallagher and Demelza Lee, at Lir Business Centre for their skill and dedication in typing up this manuscript and scanning photographs. And, finally, my grateful thanks to Maeve, Ronan and all the staff at Nonsuch Publishing.

This book is dedicated to the memory of my parents, Roy and Eileen Illingworth.

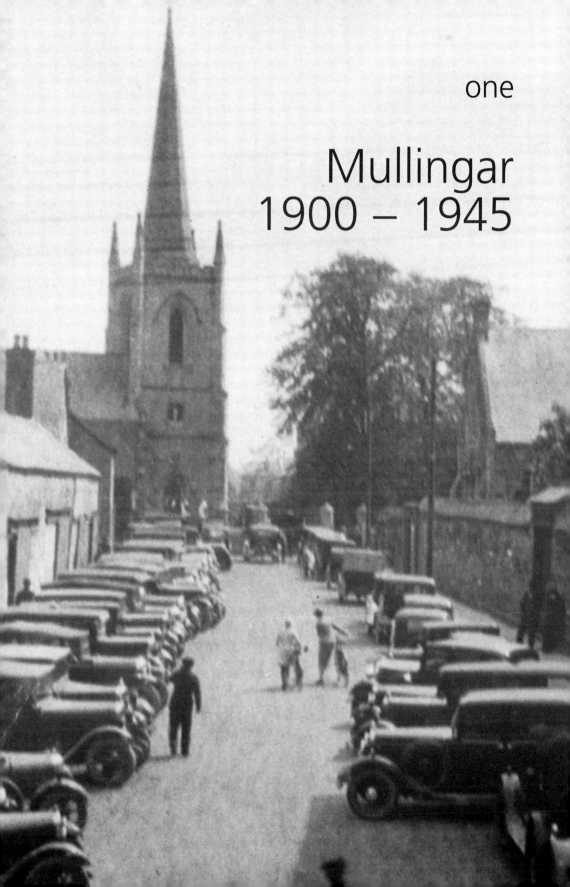

one

Mullingar
1900 – 1945

It was stated by the novelist LP Hartley that, 'The past is another country'. In the case of Mullingar, the county town of Westmeath, this is quite literally true. At the beginning of the twentieth century, Mullingar was an integral part of the United Kingdom; its citizens were subjects of Queen Victoria and British Nationals.

The Union Jack flew over the army barracks, the post boxes were red and the coins used to purchase goods had the Monarch's head on them. British soldiers played an important part in the community life of Mullingar. The majority of Mullingar people in 1900 were Nationalists who hoped for the restoration of an Irish Parliament and the maximum degree of autonomy. But very few could have imagined that within a quarter of a century they would live in an independent state.

Mullingar in 1900 was a small but reasonably prosperous market town which had been in existence for some seven centuries. It was a county and assize town, and contained a workhouse, a courthouse, a jail, army and police barracks, an asylum and county infirmary, and a railway station and canal harbour.

The population of the town at the start of the twentieth century was about 4,500. This was a drop of 800 on the 1891 census figure and led to the town's pubs closing early because of a lack of trade. The 1901 census recorded the existence of 823 inhabited and 55 uninhabited houses.

Agriculture was important for the economic life of the town in the early years of the twentieth century. Mullingar has a rich agricultural hinterland and the town had a weekly market at which butter, cheese, eggs, chickens and other farm produce were bought and sold. The butter market was particularly good, with merchants such as Andrew Hughes transporting butter to Dublin by both train and canal boat. The town also hosted a number of important fairs – particularly for horses and wool. Mullingar horse fair was one of the largest in the country. As many as nine special trains, each carrying up to 500 cattle left Mullingar every fair day. At the 1899 November horse fair, 380 wagons and 50 horseboxes were needed for the transit of stock. At the start of the century and for many decades after, the streets and squares of Mullingar would be thronged with sheep, pigs, cattle and horses as the farmers came to town.

Mullingar at the start of the 1900s had no industrial or business parks. A few small industries such as brewing and coach building existed. But most people were employed in services or institutions. The railway was a significant employer, with up to 300 employees at one stage. Other sources of work included the asylum, the infirmary and the army barracks. Although the Nationalist public representatives for the town disliked the British Army, they appreciated the economic benefits that the presence of the military brought to Mullingar, and frequently urged the War Office to increase the size of the barracks and make it a regimental depot.

In an age before supermarkets, Mullingar people bought food and other necessities from a wide variety of small, generally family-run, businesses. Trade directories and local newspapers give a sense of the wide range of businesses that existed, including butchers, bakers, dressmakers, carpenters, grocers, publicans, tailors, plumbers, watchmakers and chemists. Some businesses, such as blacksmiths and coopers, would disappear as the new century progressed. Prominent shops in early twentieth-century Mullingar included: P.J. English's Medical Hall; P.J. Weymes's Wool and Hides Business; James Tuite's Watchmakers; Nooney and Sons' Ironmongers and Hardware Store; William Gordon's Drapers; Day's Bazaar Bookshop, and Joseph Shaw's Grocery.

Queen Victoria died in 1901 and the 'Her' on official mail was changed to 'His'.

The Canal Harbour in 1900.

The Mullingar pig market in 1936.

Dominick Square sheep market.

The town also had a number of imposing bank buildings, including the Ulster Bank, built in art deco style in 1911, and a fine post office. As well as merchants, the professional class included doctors and solicitors, many drawn from the now assertive and growing Catholic middle class.

Politically, Mullingar was a Nationalist town, although labour interests predominated on the Town Commissioners. In 1898, local government reforms had led to the creation of Westmeath County Council and Mullingar Rural District Council. The RDCs, which were abolished in 1925, had functions similar to today's area committees. The first chairman of the county council was Lord Greville, who was landlord of Mullingar and lived near the town at Clonhugh House.

At first, the council met upstairs in the courthouse, but in 1913 they moved across the road to purpose-built County Buildings. The new County Buildings were built on the site of the jail. Westmeath's County Jail closed in 1900 and part of the jail complex was used for Mullingar's first vocational school. The Governor's house and some other buildings were retained and still stand today.

The General Election of 1906 brought a new political figure to the fore in Westmeath. Larry Ginnell, elected as MP for north Westmeath, was a passionate Nationalist and social radical. He began a campaign to have large ranches broken up so that grazing land could be made suitable to landless men and small holders. He began his campaign at the Downs, a few kilometres east of Mullingar, in the summer of 1906, with the slogan, 'The land for the people, the road for the bullock'. Ginnell's followers drove cattle off the lands of ranchers and landlords. The cattle driving caused immense disruption around Mullingar and elsewhere, making Ginnell deeply unpopular with many Nationalists – some of whom were themselves ranchers. John P. Hayden, editor of the local Nationalist newspaper the *Westmeath Examiner* was particularly hostile towards Ginnell and rarely gave him fair coverage in his reports on Nationalist Party meetings. However, some local politicians, such as Patrick Brett, merchant and Town Commissioner, who would later join Sinn Féin, were more sympathetic.

All Nationalists did, however, agree on the need for Irish self-government, and numerous rallies in support of Home Rule were held in and around Mullingar in the early 1900s. Cultural Nationalism was also growing in popularity. In 1901, a branch of the Gaelic League was founded in the town. On 13 July 1901, Mullingar Town Commissioners decided to have bilingual street signs. In 1902 Patrick Pearse visited Mullingar to give a talk to the local Gaelic League; the league held well-attended classes and an annual Feis was organised in the grounds of St Mary's CBS. The Christian Brothers and the Presentation Sisters were among the main supporters of the cultural revival. Gaelic football and hurling also began to become more popular, gradually replacing cricket as Mullingar's most popular sport.

Not all the people of Mullingar were Nationalists, however. About 12 per cent of the town's population was Protestant and they were largely, though not exclusively, unionist in their politics. They had not had political representation in Mullingar since the 1880s, but they did have a newspaper, *The Westmeath Guardian*, to voice their viewpoint. Unionists, like Nationalists, were drawn from all sectors of society, but were predominantly found among the local landed gentry and the professional class. They mostly kept out of local politics after 1900, but the Third Home Rule Bill did bring them out to express their opposition in the 1912-1914 period. Nor was it just the men who were involved in the unionist cause. In February 1912, a Westmeath branch of the Women's Unionist Alliance was formed in Mullingar, at a meeting in Knockdrin Castle.

Soldiers of the Connaught Rangers in Mullingar, *c.*1903.

Pearse Street around 1900.

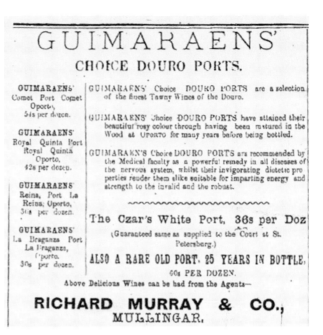

Advertisement for Richard Murray's. Note the reference to the Russian Court!

The branch unanimously passed a resolution proposed by Mrs Tottenham of Tudenham House, 'That we condemn in the most emphatic manner the introduction of any Home Rule bill, believing as we do that any such measure would bring financial and social disaster, not only to Ireland, but also to Great Britain and the Empire'.

But the Home Rule Bill could not be stopped. In May 1914, it was passed in the House of Commons for the third time, which meant that the House of Lords had to accept it. There was tremendous excitement in Mullingar, with bonfires blazing in several places and virtually every house illuminated. The Green Flag flew from the courthouse and a parade took place through the town which was attended by Joseph Dowdall, the Chairman of the County Council, and many other local politicians. Also taking part in the parade were the Mullingar Branches of the Ancient Order of Hibernians, Irish National Foresters and the Irish National Volunteers.

The Irish National Volunteers, founded by Eoin McNeill in November 1913 in Dublin, soon spread across the country, and by the summer of 1914 there were about 400 members in Mullingar. They drilled and paraded regularly and their officers included Colonel Maurice Moore, former Commandant at the army barracks. Moore was a brother of the novelist George Moore and was a supporter of Home Rule and a member of the Gaelic League.

Although the 'National Question' divided most Catholics and Protestants, community relations in Mullingar in the early 1900s were generally good. Both communities joined forces, for example, in promoting the cause of temperance – a big issue in the country at the time. Both Roman Catholic and Protestant clergy in Mullingar advocated abstinence from alcohol, with the Catholic clergy running the St Mary's Temperance Club and visiting priests running temperance missions. The Church of Ireland had a children's temperance society and the Methodists ran the Band of Hope. But attempts to supply temperance refreshments at fair days met with little success and a temperance café, set up in 1913, lasted only a year. The Mullingar Licensed Vintners Association proved more powerful than the local temperance campaigners.

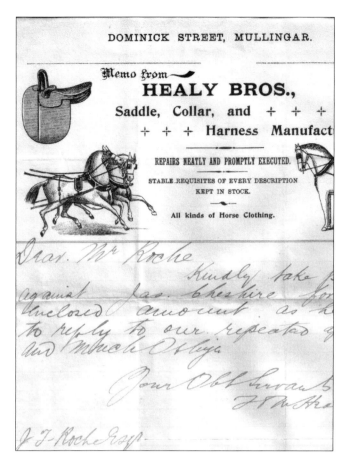

DOMINICK STREET, MULLINGAR.

Memo from —

HEALY BROS.,

Saddle, Collar, and + + +
+ + + Harness Manufact

REPAIRS NEATLY AND PROMPTLY EXECUTED.

STABLE REQUISITES OF EVERY DESCRIPTION
KEPT IN STOCK.

All kinds of Horse Clothing.

*Dear Mr Roche
Kindly take
against Jas. Cheshire for
enclosed amount as h
to reply to our repeated q
and much oblige
Your Obt Servant
...
& J. Roche Esq.*

Handbill for Healy
Brothers, 1899.

At the start of the century, the average life expectancy for Mullingar people would have been only fifty and many children and young adults died from illnesses such as Diphtheria, Tuberculosis, Scarlatin and even Dysentery. In an age without antibiotics, deaths from pneumonia and tetanus were common. Few houses had indoor toilets and there was no central heating.

But things were getting better, because in 1901, after four decades of passionate and sometimes bizarre debate on the issue, Mullingar finally got a pumping station and waterworks. No longer would the River Brosna, which flows through the town, be an open sewer, as it had been for most of the nineteenth century, and no longer would the townspeople have to rely on standpipes and old wells for their water.

By 1914, government reforms meant that Mullingar people were able to avail of welfare benefits such as unemployment assistance and old age pensions for the first time. Mullingar had an active Town Tenants' Organisation and a Working Men's Club. Many local women belonged to the Women's National Health Association, set up by the radical vicereine of Ireland, Lady Aberdeen, to educate on issues of hygiene and better health care.

Technology was changing the lives of Mullingar people by the 1910s. James Joyce, who spent time in Mullingar in 1900 and 1901, later wrote about 'The long crooked main street' of the town. In winter, the street was a quagmire of mud and manure. In summer, dust was

Invoice from Merlehan's
Victuallers, 1890.

everywhere and the Town Commissioners deployed a water cart to keep the dust at bay. But the era of horse-drawn cars, coaches and carts was coming to an end. The bicycle was an increasingly popular mode of transport for many and by 1905 there were thirteen motor cars and twenty motorcycles registered. A Mr James of Knockdrin Castle was the town's first car owner. P.W. Shaw, the Chairman of the Town Commission, and Dr Kearney of the County Infirmary were among the first owners of motorcycles. Crowds of people used to gather to watch the first motorists driving through the mud and dust clouds at ten miles per hour. Those who drove in Mullingar at this time had to abide by the requirement of the 1903 Motor Act to 'stop on signal of a restive horse when a constable or person in charge of the animal puts up his hand as a signal'. Given these restrictions, it is not surprising that, up to the First World War, most Mullingar folk continued to rely on horses and on the railway to get them around. In 1900, it took them almost an hour to travel from Mullingar to Kinnegad, so trains were the main method of transport for those travelling beyond the town. In 1900, there were six trains each way between Mullingar and Dublin daily. In a town lit by gas, Mullingar's railway station stood out as a symbol of progress when, in June 1900, electric light was installed.

According to the 1911 Census, there were 2,360 females in Mullingar. The majority of women in Mullingar were homemakers or were employed as domestic servants, teachers or shop assistants. Employment opportunities for women were very limited in the early twentieth

The promise of 'Painless Dentistry' in 1901.

The AOH was one of the leading Nationalist organisations in early 1900s Ireland.

The Irish National Foresters was another popular Nationalist association.

century. In Mullingar, the infirmary and asylum would have been significant employers of females and there were also three orders of Nuns; Presentation, Loreto and Mercy. Quite a few women ran their own businesses, such as Ann Canto who had a confectioner's on Earl Street; Mary Kelly, who ran a bookshop; Mrs Murphy, who was a dealer in china and glass, and Maryanne Sneyd, a grocer and spirit dealer.

Most surprising is the fact that, at the start of the twentieth century, Mullingar had a female dentist, a Miss Davies, whose practice was in what is now Oliver Plunkett (then Greville) Street. Dressmaking also provided many women with a living. Prostitution had been a major problem in the town in the mid-nineteenth century, but by the early 1900s the number of sex workers seem to have decreased, or at least to have been less visible.

One of Ireland's first female doctors, Ada English, was born in Mullingar. A graduate of the Royal University (now NUI) she worked in various Dublin hospitals before taking up a position in Ballinasloe Mental Hospital just before the First World War. In 1914, she would be among the founding members of Cumann na mBan. A staunch Nationalist, she was the daughter of P.J. English, a Town Commissioner whose shop 'English's Medical Hall' was one of the most prominent businesses in early-twentieth-century Mullingar. Like all property-owning women, Dr Ada English could vote from 1898 for Town Commissioners and District Councillors and from 1911 for county councils. But she could not vote in Parliamentary Elections. Numerous women in Mullingar ran businesses and involved themselves in organisations such as the Women's Health Association and the Temperance Society. But they were still far from being equal citizens.

Mullingar has long been a garrison town and as has been mentioned, the army played an important part in the social and commercial life of the town. In 1900, for example, the string band of the Cameron Highlanders provided the music at a production of *The Wicklow Wedding* put on by the Temperance Society's Drama Group, and in 1913 the String Band of the Highland light infantry played at the Westmeath Hunt Ball in the newly opened County Hall. Many of the soldiers from all over Britain who were stationed in Mullingar, such as the Manchester Regiment, actually married local women and settled in the town.

The army was also a source of employment, particularly for working-class men, and in the early 1900s Mullingar men were serving all over the British Empire in regiments such as the Leinsters and the Connaught Rangers. At the start of the century, some were fighting against the Afrikaners in South Africa in the Boer War. Nationalists in the town supported the Boers and condemned Britain, but still townspeople turned out to cheer the soldiers as they marched to the station on the way to fight in the war. The local GAA clubs banned soldiers from membership in the early 1900s, but shopkeepers welcomed their custom, local politicians took pride in the bravery of Irish Soldiers in battle, and when four soldiers died in a fire at the Barracks in 1908, the whole town mourned them.

Mullingar a century ago had no television, radio or internet to keep people informed of events in the outside world. The telegraph was the fastest method of communication and telegrams could be sent from the post office, the railway station and, on race days, from the racecourse at Newbrook. The postal service was generally highly efficient, with more than one delivery a day. From 1910, the Post Office began installing telephones in homes and businesses around the town. Early customers included the Greville Arms Hotel, the County Infirmary, the Mullingar Motor Company and J.P. Whelehan Chemist.

Lord Greville.

On Sunday 28 June 1914, hundreds of Mullingar people availed of special rail fares to attend a temperance rally in Dublin. On the same day, the heir to the Austrian Throne, Arch Duke Franz Ferdinand, was assassinated in Bosnia. Within weeks, his death had led to European war. The First World War would ruin the lives of many Mullingar people and change the course of Irish history.

The outbreak of the war on 4 August 1914, impacted on Mullingar straight away, as soldiers departed from the barracks for the front and reservists were called up. John Redmond's call for the Irish Volunteers to join the army was well responded to in Westmeath. Indeed, north Westmeath was one of the areas of highest recruitment in the entire United Kingdom. In December 1915, a recruitment meeting was held in the Greville Arms Hotel, attended by County Councillors and Town Commissioners, at which it was said that on a population bases, Mullingar had sent more men than any other town in Ireland. By then some 3,000 men from the locality of Mullingar and north Westmeath were in the services.

The local recruiting regiment was the Leinster Regiment and a Comforts Fund was set up to supply soldiers with socks, mufflers, tobacco and other items. The Comforts Fund organised concerts and bazaars and attracted much support. In January 1916, for instance, a 'Great Gift Sale' was held in the County Hall. People were urged to 'Come to the sale and help our soldiers at the front'. A goat was put up for sale and sold thirty-six times and £810 was made from this (he was eventually given to the Leinster Regiment as a mascot). The flags of Britain, France, Belgium and the other allies were flown alongside the green flag of Ireland. As far as most Mullingar people were concerned, the men serving in the war were Irish patriots who deserved the support of their town. A few in Mullingar, like Larry Ginnell MP, held different views. But as yet they were in a minority.

As well as the Leinsters, other regiments also attracted recruits including the Connaught Rangers, Royal Dublin Fusiliers and Irish Guards. Between 1914 and 1918, Mullingar men would see action in France, Belgium, Greece, Macedonia, Turkey, Iraq, Palestine and East Africa; in the air and at sea. More than fifty would never return home. Others would return with serious, sometimes permanent injuries, both physical and mental.

The Mullingar fatalities are too numerous to be detailed here, but they included Christopher Rock, Michael Rattigan, James Finlay, John Keelan, Thomas Murtagh, Patrick Bardon, Richard Keena, Michael Dunne and Thomas Harte. Three Mullingar men were killed on the first day of the Battle of the Somme alone (1 July 1916). Owen Kelly from Patrick Street, Michael Stretch from Blackhall, Michael Beglan from Austin Friars Street and Michael Farrell from

Mount Street looking south towards the County Jail, *c.*1900.

Patrick Street were also fatalities. Lieutenant Desmond Tottenham from Tudenham House at Lough Ennell was serving with the Royal Navy when he was killed at the Battle of Jutland in May 1916. One of the most tragic cases was that of Private Thomas Hope from Mill Road. He was arrested for desertion, court-martialled and executed for cowardice in March 1915 in France. He was one of some 300 British soldiers executed for 'cowardice' and other offences, posthumously pardoned by the British Government in 2007.

Few tributes to the war dead are as dignified as that which appeared in the *Westmeath Examiner* in 1916 from the mother of Mullingar soldier Private James Finlay, 'He was aged twenty-six, was a devout Catholic and held in high esteem by all who knew him. He joined the Leinsters in Mullingar in October 1915. He leaves a widowed mother and a sister to mourn him.'

Nor were all the fatalities military personnel. A Miss Doyle from Harbour Street drowned in the *Lusitania* disaster in May 1915 (her brother was later killed in Belgium).

A number of Mullingar soldiers were decorated for bravery. Almost the whole town turned out to welcome George Boyd Rochfort who had been awarded the Victoria Cross for saving the lives of his men by grabbing a mortar bomb and throwing it back out of a trench. Private R. Cully was awarded the Distinguished Conduct Medal, as were Private Thomas Leonard, Sergeant Dunne and Sapper William McLoughlin. A Private Kenny won the Military Cross, while Colonel Charles Howard Bury of Belvedere was awarded the Distinguished Service Order. The Town Commissioners Honoured Private Cully with this tribute, 'Actions such as his, bring credit to his native town, Mullingar, and still most lustre to the splendid records of the Irish Soldiers generally.'

Advertisement for Pat Brett & Co.

Dr P.J. Kearney was granted a leave of absence from Mullingar Infirmary to join the Royal Army Medical Corps. A Nurse Callan from the asylum was granted leave to work in a Red Cross Hospital in England. Fr Bernard Farrell, a curate in the cathedral, was one of many clergymen of all denominations to serve as a military chaplain. Fr Farrell served in what is now Iraq, where the campaign to drive the Turks out of their Arab Provinces was being spearheaded by Lawrence of Arabia, the son of a Westmeath man.

As well as the Leinster Regiment Comforts Fund, Mullingar people also raised funds for the Red Cross. A Red Cross Hospital for wounded officers was set up in Bloomfield House, with Mrs Locke from Kilbeggan as Matron. A convalescent home was also opened in Tudenham House.

In 1917 a Flag Day was held in the town in aid of the French Red Cross following a visit to Mullingar by a French priest who gave townspeople a vivid description of the sufferings being endured by the French and Belgian peoples. Mullingar also provided a temporary home for refugees from Belgium. 'Enemy Aliens' – German and Austrian nationals resident in Mullingar were interned.

The army barracks was an extremely busy place during the war, since Mullingar became a major training base for the thousands of men who volunteered for Field Marshal Kitchener's new army. In 1918, Mullingar became the depot for the Leinster Regiment. Soldiers trained at Newbrook racecourse, as well as at the barracks and adjoining camp field.

The 1916 Rising took the people of Mullingar completely by surprise. During Easter week, the railway station became almost a refugee camp, as all trains to Dublin were stopped at Mullingar. People slept in rooms and carriages and some were provided with food, water and money by local curate Revd Hugh Carpenter. Not until Tuesday 27 April could a special train from Clonsilla get through to take the stranded on to their destination.

With telegraph lines cut and no newspapers printed, it took several days for information on what was going on to filter out. Extra police were sent to Mullingar but the town remained quiet. The Town Commissioners held an emergency meeting at which they decided to help organise a number of citizens into a sort of home guard called the Volunteer Defence Corps to work with the RIC and the army to keep the peace, but there was little for them to do. From 2 May a curfew was in place between 8p.m. and 5a.m. and the army were on duty at the Market House accompanied by local police. Only doctors and clergy were exempt from the curfew.

Mullingar Town Commission, along with the District and County Councils, roundly condemned the Rising. So did the editor of the *Westmeath Examiner*, John P. Hayden, who saw the rebellion as an attack on John Redmond and the Home Rule Movement, which would undermine the Nationalist cause. In his editorial, he stated that, 'The past week has added a dark and bitter chapter to the history of Ireland', and added, 'The recent Rising was promoted by persons who had a deep aversion to Constitutional Effort.'

Although they condemned the Rising, local politicians and clergy also urged mercy for the rebels and criticised the executions. Larry Ginnell spoke out passionately against the death sentences and harried the Prime Minister and other Ministers with questions about the treatment of Irish prisoners. By the autumn of 1916, Mullingar's MP was himself a prisoner and was sentenced to six months.

Those killed during the Rising included Mullingar man Thomas Hickey and his son, both of whom were murdered by British troops in North King Street, and a brother of Miss Hevey who worked in Patrick Brett's shop in Greville Street who was 'killed during the disturbances when he was leaving his burning house in Moore Street'. Dr Ada English, Town Commissioner, acted as Medical Officer to the Irish Volunteers involved with the Rising at Athenry, Co. Galway.

For ardent young Nationalists in Mullingar like Michael McCoy, the Easter Rising was an inspiring but frustrating event because of the lack of action in Westmeath. But their day would soon come. In 1917, the tide of opinion began to shift in favour of Sinn Féin and other radical Nationalists. A Prisoners' Aid Fund, set up to raise money to help the families of those executed and imprisoned, attracted widespread support in Mullingar. Fr Hugh Carpenter, the cathedral administrator, allowed a fundraising concert to take place in the County Hall on a Sunday night. In 1917, a major Sinn Féin rally took place in Mullingar attended by Eamon de Valera, Arthur Griffith, Ada English and others. Larry Ginnell became the first Irish Party MP to defect to Sinn Féin. Resolutions were passed by the local councils calling for the release of all Republican prisoners and deploring the death on hunger strike of Thomas Ashe.

By 1917 the war was going badly, with mounting casualties and growing economic hardship. Although farmers were doing well, the poorer people of the town were going hungry, with inflation eating into their meagre incomes. Vegetables, milk and meat were scarce, as was coal, which led to rationing of street lighting. More and more young people began to see the war as 'England's Problem' and Sinn Féin gained numerous recruits. The National Irish Volunteers who had disagreed with John Redmond's support for the war, now began to reorganise themselves as the Irish Republican Army (IRA), and the IRB also recruited. The Mullingar

Knockdrin Castle, where the Westmeath Ladies Unionist Association was formed in 1912.

Above: Lady Aberdeen Cottages, built in 1908.

Right: A Mullingar business woman in early 1900s.

Below: The Soldiers' Home at the Fair Green in the early 1900s.

Volunteers were known as Mullingar Company and eventually became a battalion within the midlands brigade of the IRA. A jeweller in Mullingar called David Burke recruited people to both the IRB and to the intelligence section of the IRA. Weapons began to be acquired, including rifles handed over by Irishmen serving in the British Army, and preparations for some kind of guerrilla warfare started. The widespread opposition to Britain's attempt to impose conscription on Ireland added to the growing Nationalist fervour in Mullingar, with Nationalists of all kinds and local priests condemning the move and signing petitions opposing conscription and pledging resistance. In April 1918, an anti-conscription rally attracted 10,000 people.

As the First World War drew to an end in 1918, Ireland, like the rest of the world, was ravaged by a violent flu pandemic known as Spanish flu. It killed up to 50 million people worldwide with 20,000 dying in Ireland. At a meeting of Mullingar Rural District Council in October 1918, the MOH, Dr T.J. Daly, delivered a bleak warning:

> I cannot hold myself responsible for the treatment of the sick, poor, during the existence of the present plague and if the guardians do not appoint a doctor to give temporary assistance, I fear patients will die whose lives could be saved if they got proper attention.

The flu claimed many lives in the town (including Senior County Council Official, Michael Garry) and led to the closure of schools and businesses. A local priest asked that people offer up the national novena to God, for relief from the pandemic.

In December 1918, a general election was held following the end of the war. For the first time, all men over twenty-one in Mullingar and all property-owning women over thirty, could vote for their MP. This huge new electorate, plus much use of Nationalist rhetoric, led to Larry Ginnell winning a resounding victory over the Irish Party candidate, local merchant and councillor, P.J. Weymes (whose business contracts with the British military didn't help).

By the summer of 1919, with the War of Independence underway, town commissioners and district councillors were pledging allegiance to Dáil Éireann and the local RIC were suffering boycotts. There was a brief interlude from politics and conflict in June 1919, however, when most of the town went to the railway station to cheer the first transatlantic pilots, Alcock and Brown, as they passed through Mullingar on their way from Galway to Dublin.

In June 1920, Sinn Féin and Labour took control of all the local councils in Westmeath, following local elections. In August 1920, Westmeath County Council withdrew all co-operation from British controlled departments of government. The town commissioners too began to flex Nationalist muscles. They decided to rename the streets of Mullingar in honour of the patriot dead and other suitable persons. A few of the names took hold; Greville Street's transformation into Oliver Plunkett Street was widely welcomed, at least by Roman Catholics, and Military Road became Ashe Road, in honour of Thomas Ashe, without much controversy. The murder of Cork's Sinn Féin Lord Mayor, Thomas McCurtain, by Crown Forces in 1920, likewise brought about the renaming of Barrack Street in his honour. But it would be fifty years before Earl Street finally became Pearse Street, and some names, such as 'Republican Drive' (Springfield), Archbishop Mannix Road (Lynn Road), and O'Donovan Rossa (Harbour Street) were never accepted.

On the streets of Mullingar the RIC increasingly gave way to IRA volunteers who adopted

A social gathering at the army barracks in the 1880s.

the title 'Republican Police'. The first Sinn Féin Court was held in the town in August 1920, with local professional men serving as judges. The 'Black and Tans' took over the RIC Barracks in College Street and, in November 1920, they raided the County Council offices and seized documents including the minute book. Patrick Brett and another Mullingar man, Henry O'Brien, vice chairman of the County Council, were among the many local councillors and commissioners arrested at this time. It became increasingly difficult for local government to function at all in Mullingar.

Many local men and women risked their lives and liberty to help the national cause. Members of the Mullingar IRA included: James Hynes, who used his job as a Post Office clerk to break into RIC Ciphers; Pat Byrne, who was OC of the IRA prisoners in London's Pentonville Prison and went on hunger strike; Ed Hynes; James Coleman; Patrick Dowling; Joseph Farrell; Joseph Gavin; Lawrence Madden; Michael Madden; Patrick Ryan; John Tone; Fred Turner; John Willis; Sean Crogan; Tony Stanley, and Joseph Tormey. Thomas Foskin, a RIC sergeant who was personal clerk to the RIC County inspector, passed the cipher codes on to James Hynes and David Burke.

The OC of the Mullingar battalion was Michael McCoy, who was imprisoned several times and went on hunger strike. By 1920, Mullingar also had a branch of Cumann na mBan, whose role included supplying safe houses and first aid to the volunteers, moving weapons from place to place and gathering intelligence. Anne McDonnell, for example, used her position as a chambermaid in the Greville Arms Hotel, to spy on the army personnel who patronised the hotel.

The married quarters at the military barracks in the early 1900s.

Despite the strong Nationalist feeling in the town and incidents of sabotage against military fuel supplies, Mullingar remained a surprisingly safe place for British soldiers. The East Yorkshire regiment was stationed in the barracks for most of the War of Independence and, apart from a brawl with some Sinn Féin youths in the town centre in July 1919 and some graffiti on the walls, they encountered little overt antagonism, although some railway workers refused to drive trains carrying troops or military equipment. Indeed they got the impression that the town seemed 'well disposed to the troops'. The barracks was too important to the local economy to attract much hostility. In March 1921, Sean McEoin, the Longford–Westmeath IRA Commander, was arrested by British soldiers at Mullingar station. He tried to escape down Dominick Street, at the top of the station yard, but he was shot and wounded. He was taken to the military barracks where he was treated for his injuries before being sent to Dublin for court martial. He would make a triumphant return to Mullingar later in the year.

In May 1921, Mullingar voters re-elected Larry Ginnell to the second Dáil. Two months later, the truce ended the War of Independence. Patrick Brett was among the many prisoners given a hero's welcome when they were finally released from Ballykinlar and other camps and prisons. In September 1921, Sean McEoin was the guest of honour at a Sinn Féin dinner held in Mullingar. The guests included Eamon de Valera, Harry Boland, Michael Collins, Dr Kathleen Lynn, Margaret Pearse and Dr Ada English. Dr English had herself spent six months in Galway jail for her Cumann na mBan activities. She was now a member of the second Dáil. Michael Collins and his bodyguards stayed with Thomas Shaw in Belzize House on the Dublin Road during his visits to Mullingar.

The Anglo-Irish Treaty was largely welcomed by Mullingar politicians and people, with the Town Commission and the County Council urging local TDs to ratify it. Following the setting up of the provisional government in January 1922, the RIC disbanded and the British Army

British soldiers' graves in Ballyglass.

prepared to end its centuries-old presence in the town. In a very low key ceremony on 13 February, the Sussex regiment (who had taken over from the East Yorks just a couple of weeks earlier) handed the barracks over to Captain C.S. Todd Andrews and Brigadier S. McGuire. In June, the RIC, who had used the army barracks as a motor depot for disbandment, held a big parade before withdrawing from the town; some people saluted them as they departed. In September the first Gardaí (or Civic Guards as they were then known) arrived in Mullingar. Other signs of the new political order included the ending of the workhouse system and its replacement with the name County Home, and the announcement by the Post Office in April that the British stamps would be overprinted with the stamp 'Rialtas Seandac na h'Éireann' (Provisional Government of Ireland).

Not all Mullingar people supported the Treaty, however, and by late spring violent incidents were on the increase as anti-treaty members (known as 'irregulars') and pro-treaty forces fought for the control of the barracks in April 1922. The irregulars managed to seize control of the County Buildings and courthouse and the RIC barracks. A gun battle in Mary Street led to the deaths of pro-treaty army officer Patrick Columb (after whom the army barracks is now named), and an irregular, Joseph Leavy. Negotiations brought about a peaceful withdrawal from the County Buildings and the courthouse. The irregulars did, however, blow up the RIC barracks, causing much damage to local buildings. The noise of the explosion could be heard up to four miles away and the barracks burned fiercely, with a local paper describing how 'the large and numerous windows were veritable sheets of fire'. No one was killed or seriously injured, however, and several valuable horses were rescued from stables at the rear of the barracks.

By July, Civil War was raging and many local men were involved in the fighting around the country. A Private Gavigan from Mill Road was killed while serving in the Free State forces in Cork in August 1922. In September 1922, a Mass was held in the cathedral for the repose of the souls of Arthur Griffith and Michael Collins.

Anti-treaty forces repeatedly attacked the railway system in Westmeath during the Civil War. Trains were derailed and signal boxes blown up or burned – including one near Loreto School. To protect the network, the army set up a railway protection and maintenance corps, which was based in Mullingar. The corps used an armoured train which was named Tutankamun in honour of the recently discovered Egyptian Pharaoh.

In March 1923, two irregulars, Luke Burke and Michael Creary, were shot by firing squad in the army barracks for armed robbery. Priests from the cathedral attended them in their final hours and rushed forward to give them absolution after the shooting. These were the first and last executions to take place in twentieth-century Mullingar.

Waterworks around the country came under attack during the Civil War and to guard against such an incident in Mullingar, Free State soldiers were deployed to protect the waterworks at the end of Mill Road. No attack did take place but, in one tragic incident, a young soldier on guard duty bled to death after another soldier accidentally shot him.

Anne MP Smithson, the popular novelist, was arrested in Mullingar while smuggling supplies for the irregulars through the town. She was briefly detained at the military barracks before being sent on her way – minus the weapons. An irregular soldier was shot dead at an army checkpoint on the Main Street and many other irregulars were imprisoned in the barracks.

In one ugly incident, a number of Protestant businesses in Mullingar had their windows smashed and Protestant farmers were told to get out of Westmeath. The attacks were widely

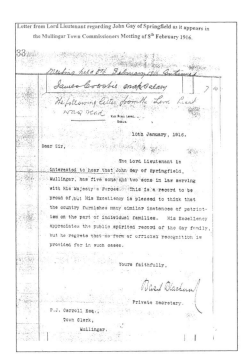

Letter from Lord Lieutenant regarding John Gay of Springfield as it appears in the Mullingar Town Commissioners Meeting of 8th February 1916.

Left: A letter to John Gay, who had seven sons serving in the armed forces in the First World War.

Right: A fundraiser event for Bloomfield Red Cross Hospital during the First World War.

condemned by the majority of townspeople and were untypical of Mullingar – a town much less divided on religious lines than many others at the time. In the aftermath of the Civil War and the British departure, the Protestant population of the town did begin to fall. The Presbyterian and Methodist communities appear to have been particularly affected by the departure of British regiments and the RIC. But most Protestants were well integrated and decided to stay. One who did was Charles Howard Bury of Belvedere who, in 1921, had made international headlines when he led the first reconnaissance of Mount Everest.

On 6 December 1922, the Irish Free State came into existence and, after almost 122 years, Mullingar ceased to be a British town. In May 1923, to the relief of Mullingar people, the Civil War ended. A month earlier, Mullingar's long-serving MP and TD, Larry Ginnell, had died in Washington, aged seventy-one. Mullingar's political representatives now included local businessman P.W. Shaw, who supported the Treaty.

With the end of the Civil War and the establishment of the Free State, the task of nation building could now begin. The tricolour now flew over the army barracks and the courthouse. The post boxes were painted green and a new Garda Station opened on the site of the old RIC Barracks. Irish became an increasingly important subject in the curriculum of Mullingar schools, with the Christian Brothers and the Presentation Sisters at the forefront of efforts to bring up a new Irish-speaking generation in the town. On St Patrick's Day 1923, the *Westmeath Examiner* launched a campaign urging Mullingar people to show their patriotism by buying Irish-made goods. The town became more overtly Roman Catholic as well; from 1927 a Corpus Christi procession was held through the town centre, with papal flags prominently displayed.

The names of saints were given to new housing developments or existing ones, such as St

Anthony's Cottages, St Finian's Terrace, St Andrew's Terrace and Trinity Cottages. The Garrison chapel at the army barracks was reconsecrated as a Roman Catholic church. The closure in 1928 of north Westmeath's Protestant and Unionist newspaper *The Westmeath Guardian* was perhaps a sign of the changing order.

New technologies began to make their appearance in Mullingar in the 1920s. By the end of the decade, the motor car was replacing the horse-drawn cars and carts.

The radio or 'wireless' became a part of many homes, with primitive crystal sets in use by the mid-1920s. The cinema had been a part of the entertainment scene since just before the First World War, and from the early 1930s Mullingar folk were able to hear, as well as see, their favourite film stars.

The Great Depression of the early 1930s hit Mullingar as hard as other places, and the Anglo-Irish Economic War of 1934-38 exacerbated the economic problems, as it hit many of the larger farmers around the town particularly hard. The army barracks had all but closed by the early thirties and this too hurt the local economy.

Relief came with a major building programme in the town. In 1932 a Greyhound Stadium opened and in the same year work began on a new GAA stadium. During the building of this stadium, the workers went on strike to demand higher pay. They were sacked and replaced with workers from other parts of the county and from Longford. The sacked workers attacked their replacements with a variety of weapons and there were pitched battles which, on one occasion unique to Mullingar, was broken up by Gardaí firing shots in the air. The problem was eventually resolved and the new Cusack Park Stadium opened on 16 July 1933. GAA clubs from across Westmeath paraded through the town and at the start of the first match the ball was thrown from an airplane.

Also in 1932, work began on building a new cathedral in the town, 'one worthy of the large and historic Diocese of Meath'. Strike action again disrupted the building work, but in July 1936, the new Cathedral of Christ the King was opened. The cathedral was consecrated on 30 August 1939 and the occasion was marked by a ceremony on Sunday 3 September, in the presence of the Irish Roman Catholic hierarchy, overseas prelates and members of the government, led by Eamon de Valera. It was a happy occasion in the town's history, with the town 'Gorgeously decorated with a great variety of flags and bunting, papal flags and colours were flown from every house without exception of creed, as all felt it was a day upon which Mullingar had reason to rejoice.'

In 1936, the 160-year-old county infirmary was replaced by a new county hospital. The former infirmary of the workhouse became a TB Hospital. The Mercy Nuns, in Mullingar since 1898, ran both the county hospital and the county home (the former workhouse) until the 1970s.

Health services were gradually improving for the people of Mullingar and the quality of housing was also improving, with new developments going up. But there was still terrible poverty in Mullingar, as elsewhere, during the thirties, and diseases such as TB and Diphtheria continued to claim lives prematurely.

In 1937, electric light came to Mullingar. The first building lit with electricity had been the railway station, which had its own generator. Now the Parochial Hall in Church Avenue was lit as well and soon private homes and businesses too. It marked the end of the gasworks, which had stood along Mill Road and Spoutwell or Gas Lane for eighty years, with its 65ft high gasometer.

REMARKABLE FEAT.

The Atlantic Crossed in Less than 17 Hours.

Brief Description of Pilot and Navigator.

CAPTAIN ALCOCK, aged 27, bachelor, started life as a shop boy in Manchester motor works, and is said to have relatives in the South of Ireland. Became a flyer at 20. Won D.S.C. as aviator on Turkish front. Was captured and held prisoner till close of war. He is modest, handsome, confident, resolute and clever. Yet no girl has yet made any impression on him.

LIEUT. BROWN, aged 33, engaged to be married to an Irish lady, was born in Glasgow of American parents. Began his engineering career at 16. Joined R.F.C. as observer, and was captured by the Germans. He was wounded, and still walks with a limp. He is very popular with numerous friends, and is a very keen observer.

Above: A Sinn Féin rally outside the County Hall *c.*1917.

Left: Alcock and Brown in June 1919. Alcock is holding a model plane given to them by a Mullingar man.

Opposite, above: Michael McCoy reads the proclamation at the Easter Sunday Commemoration in 1952.

Opposite, below: Members of Mullingar company, Old IRA, attending a plaque unveiling in CBS in 1959.

OLD I.R.A. GROUP   28 Nov 1959

Group taken on the occasion of the unveiling of the plaque (presented by the Mullingar Old I.R.A., in memory of deceased Comrades) at the C.B.S. new Primary School in Mullingar. Seated (left to right)—Joseph Fitzsimons, Lynn, Francis Smith, Mullingar, John McDermott, do. (Treasurer); Thomas Eggerton, The Downs, James Coleman, Mullingar, Roddy Faulkner, The Downs, Nicholas McCabe, Clonmore, Joseph Gavin, Robinstown, Joseph Fox, Lynn, Patk. Byrne, Mullingar. Standing (left to right)—Michael Madden, Mullingar, William McCann, Cullion, Christopher Fagan, Mullingar, Owen Dalton, The Downs, Samuel Austin, Grange, Francis Dunleavy, Mullingar, Gregory Murray, Cullion, Christopher Quinn, Ginnell Terrace, Patrick Ryan, Mullingar, Christopher Glennon, Ballinderry, Patrick Dowling, Mullingar, Joseph Farrell, Ballinea, Edward Hynes (Hon. Secretary), Mullingar; Michael McCoy (Chairman), Mullingar; John Tone Mullingar, Laurence Madden, do., Thomas Reeves, do.

The replacement of 'O.H.M.S.' by 'Rialtas Sealadach na h'Éireann' marks the end of British Rule in 1922.

One of the most dramatic events in Mullingar during the thirties was the Great Blizzard of February 1933. For several days the town was blanketed in snow drifts metres deep. Cars virtually disappeared under the snow and, near the town, a pedestrian stumbled over an abandoned bus completely buried in drifts. People were trapped on trains between Mullingar and other towns and funerals had to be postponed. Food supplies ran short in some areas and the teachers and senior boys at St Finian's College had to go out with shovels to clear a path from the school to the town, while Council workers battled through snow drifts to help get essential food and fuel supplies to the infirmary and the asylum.

THE SECOND WORLD WAR

With the outbreak of the Second World War, the army returned in force to the barracks. The soldiers who arrived in the autumn of 1939 had to clear out cattle and horse manure from the parade ground left over from the use of the place as a cattle pound during the economic war. Dilapidated buildings also had to be repaired. The army spent the severe winter of 1939/40 under canvas in the barrack square. Gradually the place was made suitable for human habitation again. In 1943, the 4th Field Artillery Regiment arrived. Mullingar also became the

Members of the Railway Protection and Maintenance Corps at the railway station in 1923.

base for the 4th Field Company Supply and Transport and the 9th (FCA) Artillery Regiment, which was set up just after the war. With fears of a German or British invasion of Ireland in 1940/41 preparations were made to blow up the canal and railway bridges, and trenches were dug to act as tank traps. Local IRA members and supporters were interned in the Curragh.

As well as the barracks, the army also took over the Old Infirmary Building, the Market House and Knockdrin Castle close to the town. The Infirmary served first as HQ for a Field Ambulance Company and then for the HQ of the Reinforced Brigade. The gate lodge was used as a guardroom and brigade commanders occupied an office.

Young men in Ireland were encouraged to become part-time soldiers in the newly formed LDF and LSF. Scores of men responded to the appeal, while women joined the Red Cross and St John Ambulance Brigade. Events such as 'Brigade Week' and 'Step Together' week saw thousands of these volunteers, as well as the regular soldiers, parading through Mullingar. On one occasion, the Taoiseach, Eamon de Valera came to town to inspect the troops during Brigade Week. Special religious services were held to honour the troops, with Roman Catholic Bishop Dr D'Alton blessing the pennants and colours in Cusack Park.

Funds raised during 'Brigade Week' went to the Mullingar Army and LDF Comforts Fund Association. The Association, whose Secretary was Miss Mairead Shaw, worked out of the Market House. Members of the Armed Forces were able to use the Market House for recreations such as darts, board games, card games and reading.

MOURNING AND PRAYING

Memory of Two Great Irish Leaders

Honoured In Mullingar

Impressive Religious, Civilian and Military Spectacles.

Solemn Requiem Service

For Late President Griffith, and General Collins

By Direction Of The Bishop.

Business Suspended During Service.

Immense Attendance—Clerical and Lay.

Mass for Michael Collins and Arthur Griffith in September 1922.

IN LOVING MEMORY OF
MICHAEL GREALY
GRANAHAN
EXECUTED IN MULLINGAR
13TH MARCH 1923 AGED 28 YEARS
HIS BROTHER **MALACHY**
DIED 13TH APRIL 1963
HIS WIFE **BRIDGET**
DIED 6TH JAN 1924

R. I. P.

GREALY

Grave of one of the two men executed in Mullingar barracks during the Civil War.

Above: The first letter to carry the postmark 'An Muileann Cearr', in 1923.

Below: Banners in place for the Corpus Christi procession in 1927.

Talking films come to Mullingar, 1932.

GAA clubs parade through Mullingar to celebrate the opening of Cusack Park in 1933.

Workers who helped build the cathedral, pictured in 1939.
Back row, left to right: John Corscadden, Michael Madden, John Farrelly, Michael Byrne, Michael Kelly, Jack Boland, Owen McGrath.
Front row: Patrick Coffey, Johnny Crowley, Patsy Cleary, Jimmy Scally, Johnny Weymes, 'Jazzer' Mulligan, Joe Fitzgerald, Bill Scally.

A view across Mullingar from the Dublin Bridge in 1936. This would have been one of the first photographs to show the newly completed cathedral.

The new County Hospital in 1936.

Dr Tony Stanley, a local GP, played an important part in Mullingar's war effort. A veteran of the War of Independence and a noted playwright and amateur actor, he put his various talents at the disposal of the town during the war. He and his wife Margaret were among the founders of the Mullingar Branch of the Red Cross in 1939 and Dr Stanley ran first aid classes for the LDF, LSF and St John Ambulance. He also organised plays and pageants for brigade week to raise funds for the Comforts Fund.

A number of local men and women served in the allied army forces during the war. Anthony Tottenham from Tudenham joined the RAF in 1942. In September 1944, he was killed when his plane was shot down over France. His remains are buried in Wissant Military Cemetery near Calais. He was just twenty-one when he was killed. He was posthumously awarded the Distinguished Flying Cross.

His brother Nicholas and father Harold also served in the war and both were captured by the Japanese, Nicholas in Java and Harold in Malaysia. In an episode worthy of a Hollywood movie, father and son were reunited in a Japanese Camp at Changi, Singapore in 1943. Both survived two years of harsh treatment by the Japanese, and Major Tottenham, who had also served in the First World War, returned to Mullingar after the war.

Another Mullingar man, William Harvey-Kelly, served in the Irish Guards and took part in the D-day landings. A number of Mullingar men living in Britain were conscripted into

Left: An invoice from the Gasworks.
Right: Pat Carroll, Mullingar Fire Officer, in uniform.

the Armed Forces and saw military service in Italy, France, North Africa, Burma, the Far East and at sea. Many others did vital war work in British factories and hospitals. A number of Westmeath-born people were killed in air raids in Britain, including a Miss Daly from Mullingar.

The war meant that Ireland was faced with food and fuel shortages as imports dried up. P.J. Bartely, the government-appointed Commissioner who was running Westmeath following the dissolution of the County Council in 1935 for failing to strike a rate, summed up the crisis facing Ireland, 'It is clear now it will be an impossibility to get anything from outside into this country.'

In Mullingar, bicycles and horse-drawn transport replaced motor cars on the streets. Train journeys to and from the town could take all day due to fuel shortages, and bus services were cut back from seven days to five. Peat was cut and burned in place of coal.

With a real threat of hunger due to restrictions on food imports, every available piece of land was utilised for food production. Farmers around Mullingar received orders for compulsory tillage. The Catholic Bishop turned the cathedral grounds over for the growing of cabbage, carrots, lettuce and other vegetables. Anything that could be recycled was. It was a testing time for the town but Mullingar pulled through and, for most people, life went on much as before, with little realisation of what the war was really like.

4th Field Artillery with new 105mm guns at the army barracks, 1998.

Stand down parade for the European Army at the Barracks, 1945.

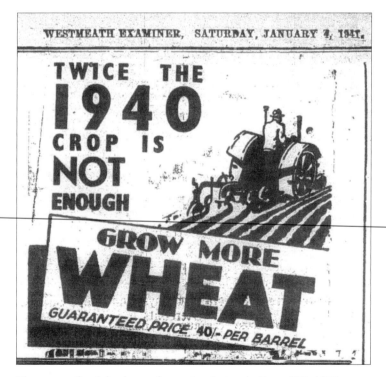

The country faced the threat of starvation during the Second World War.

two

Mullingar
Since the War

The post-war years were a difficult time for Mullingar – employment was scarce and there was little in the way of industry. In 1936, in an effort to encourage local industry and source employment, the government set up a pencil factory. The factory, which remained operational until 1955, was situated in the army barrack, and was the only one of its kind in the country. But for many years after the war, local politicians and newspapers would spend much time begging the government and businesses to bring industry to the town. 'Mullingar needs a factory', was the cry, year after year.

In 1946, large numbers of young people from Mullingar volunteered to go out into the countryside to help local farmers save the harvest following an exceptionally wet summer. With food scarce across Europe in the aftermath of war, there was real fear of hunger if the harvest was not saved. The weather was not kind in those times, for the wet summer of 1946 was followed by the long, bitterly cold winter of 1947 and Mullingar people struggled with shortages of fuel. With unemployment high, some young men found work and pay in the ranks of the Mullingar battalion of the FCA, which was formed in January 1947.

There was great excitement in Mullingar in 1947 when a film, *Captain Boycott*, was partly filmed at the Newbrook racecourse. Several locals got work as extras and it was said that some girls earned so much more on the film set than they had done as domestic servants, that they never returned to their jobs!

There was more excitement in the town in 1948 when some children apparently claimed to have seen a vision of Mary at Gaybrook, just south of the town. For a few days people came from far and wide to see the vision. But the local clergy were sceptical and the 'Gaybrook vision' was soon quietly forgotten.

One important visitor to Mullingar just after the war was the newly created Cardinal, John Glennon, Archbishop of St Louis in the USA. Cardinal Glennon was of Westmeath birth, had been educated at St Mary's CBS in Mullingar and preached at its dedication and consecration. Most of the town turned out to honour him when he passed through on his way to Rome. Just a few weeks after his visit he died in Dublin and his body lay in state in Mullingar Cathedral for two days before a funeral Mass attended by three Cardinals, the President, the Taoiseach and other dignitaries.

In February 1951, a group of local Irish music and language enthusiasts met in the Midland Hotel in Mullingar to found Comhaltas Ceoltóirí Éireann. The aim of Comhaltas was to promote Irish music, song and dance and to look after the interest of musicians, dancers and singers. Mullingar families such as the Moynihans and Mulreadys were among the founders of what remains one of Ireland's most important cultural organisations. The first Comhaltas Feis took place in Mullingar in May of that year and attracted many of the country's finest traditional musicians.

Throughout the 1950s, employment was scarce in Mullingar. Those who had work locally regularly worked very long hours, often at backbreaking manual jobs with poor pay. Each year, hundreds of young people emigrated to Britain and other lands in search of employment. In the early 1950s, some Mullingar men went to Canada to mine uranium on the edges of the Arctic Circle. Those who returned to Ireland would later start local businesses such as The Yukon Bar and the Lake County Hotel with the money they earned in the mines. Others went to the USA and Australia but by far the largest number went to Britain. The trains to Dublin in the fifties became known as 'Lizzie's Trains', as whole families moved to England.

ESTABLISHED 1936

Manufacturers of

PENS
PENCILS
CRAYONS

"Graphic" and "Meteor" black lead pencils, "Angelo" Drawing pencils in various degrees. "Dexter" round coloured Checking pencils. "Trident" large hexagon Checking pencils. "Diabolo" Copying pencils. Medium, Hard, Extra Hard, Red, Blue and Magenta colours. "Cashel" crayons in 12 colours. Eyebrow and Manicure pencils. Carpenter's and Advertising pencils. Diary pencils and pens of various descriptions. See the name PENCEIRE on all our pencils.

SUPPLIERS TO HOME AND EXPORT TRADE
ALL OUR PRODUCTS ARE MANUFACTURED FROM FINEST MATERIALS
IN OUR FACTORY AT MULLINGAR.

PENCILS (IRELAND) LIMITED
PENCEIRE MILLS
MULLINGAR, Co. Westmeath, IRELAND

Telephone: Mullingar 25   Telegrams: Pencils, Mullingar.
3328

Town Commissioners' House Transfers

INCREASED RENTS SUGGESTION

A suggestion by Mr. McGeeney, Co. Manager—that where transfers are granted to the Old Town Commissioners' houses the rents be increased—was made at the March meeting of the Commissioners on Thursday night.

He further suggested that in the meantime no transfers be considered. The Commissioners decided to adjourn consideration of the matter until the figures are circulated, and the transfers will continue in the interim.

The proposed increases are: (existing rent in first place, proposed increases in second):—
St. Andrew's Tce.,—3/-, plus rates, proposed increase to 5/- plus rates.
Parnell Tce. — Nine at 3/-, four at 2/6, proposed increase to 5/- in all cases.
St. Loman's Tce.—5/-, proposed increase to 8/-.
McEoin's Terrace — 8/6 proposed increase to 12/-.
St. Lawrence's Tce.—5/- proposed increase to 7/6.
St. Finlan's Tce., to be left as at present:
Grand Parade Tce.—9/6, 9/- and 7/-; proposed increase to 10/-, 10/- and 8/-.
Cathedral View—4/6 and 3/-, proposed increase to 8/-.
St. Brigid's Tce.—9/-, 7/6 and 4/-, proposed increase to 12s. 9s., and 6/-.

Mr. Shaw suggested that the figures be circulated and also details of the economic rents.

Mr. Mitchell asked if the houses are a liability.

Mr. McGeeney said all the houses are a liability. He stated that the rents are much too low.

Mr. Coleman said that in connection with the proposed purchase schemes the Minister sent down a circular in which it was stated that they would have power to increase the rents in cases of those not purchasing. He felt that they should take no action about increased rent until all the purchase schemes were put into operation and the results

known.

Mr. Dowling said he had proposed before that in the case of a person whose income exceeds £7 he should not be transferred into a cheaper Terrace.

Mr. O'Callaghan said that such a person might be leaving a cheaper cottage available.

Mr. McGeeney said that such points are always borne in mind. He stated that with the sale of cottages in Longford and Westmeath to tenants the idea of having rents increased on those who do not purchase had been approved.

CONDOLENCE.

On the proposition of the Chairman votes of sympathy were passed with the relatives of the late Mr. Joseph Bennett and with Mr. Begian on the death of his sister.

PUBLIC LIGHTING.

The meeting approved an expenditure of £32 5/- in connection with improved lighting at the Jail Hill, the Parochial Hall, on the Dublin Road, at Blackhall and Cathedral View.

WEEKLY MARKET.

The Chamber of Commerce and R.G.D.A.T.A. have agreed that as a trial for this year, when a holiday falls on a Thursday (there will be two such instances this year) the market will be held on Wednesday of that week, instead of on Friday.

The Commissioners agreed to make arrangements to this effect.

PIGS BOUGHT LIVE-
WEIGHT
EVERY THURSDAY
BEFORE 11 A.M.
Weighed and paid for on the spot.
MORAN'S STORES,
RATHOWEN.

Above: Mullingar Pencil Factory advertisement from 1950.

Left: House rents set by Town Commission, 1954.

Despite the poor state of the economy and the very real poverty, Mullingar remained a lively place, with thriving theatre companies, musical societies and sports clubs. In April 1955, a locally trained horse, 'Quare Times', won the English Grand National. The horse was led in triumphant procession through the town from the Dublin Road to the Green Bridge and the Town Commissioners honoured the trainer, Mrs Wellman. A party was held in the Greville Arms Hotel at which Rex Beaumont of Belvedere, who owned a sibling of 'Quare Times', read out a telegram of congratulations to 'Quare Times, from his brother'!

In 1958, Mullingar Cathedral witnessed a significant musical event; the Irish premiere of Elgar's *Dream of Gerontius*, performed by the Hallé Orchestra of Manchester, conducted by Sir John Barbirolli. The President of Ireland, Seán T. O'Kelly, was present for the performance.

In 1955, Ireland had joined the United Nations and, from 1958, Ireland began to deploy troops on peacekeeping duties. Colonel Michael O'Donnell from Mullingar served in Kashmir in 1958, but the first large-scale deployment of troops from Mullingar was to the Congo in 1960.

A total of twenty-seven soldiers from Columb Barracks volunteered for service with the 32nd Irish Battalion. Those who went included: M.J. Carroll, Springfield; M.T. Cahill, Cathedral View; T. Creevy, Patrick Street; P.J. Hegarty, St Anthony's Cottages; J. Harney, St Finian's Terrace; P. Kelly, Cathedral View; T. Nooney, Gas Lane; T. Scally, Ginnell Terrace; W. Archibold, Springfield; W. Nally, College Street; M.J. Seery, Ginnell Terrace; T. Hegarty, St Anthony's Cottages; O. Creevy, Cathedral View, and F. Newman, Harbour Street. Military service in the Congo would continue for several years and one particular part of Mullingar, St Finian's Terrace, at the barracks, became known as 'Congo Terrace' because so many UN Veterans lived there. Mullingar troops also served in Cyprus during the 1960s.

At the start of the 1960s, Mullingar was still quite a small town, its population standing at 5,900 in 1961. The sixties would see a rise in that population as some industry and greater prosperity finally arrived.

In 1962, Mullingar Creamery was opened, following on from the success of a milk separating station opened in 1960. In 1968, local entrepreneur Ted O'Leary (father of Michael O'Leary) founded Tailteann Textiles Knitwear factory, which, by 1963, was employing sixty people. Other factories would later follow and the town finally began to acquire an industrial base.

There was no construction boom in mid-century Mullingar. In 1963, it made news when fifteen new houses were built. But from the late 1940s onwards, private housing schemes began and by the mid sixties a number of new estates with good quality housing had opened, including Ginnell Terrace and O'Growney Drive. In June 1963, Fleadh Cheoil na hÉireann took place in Mullingar over the Whit Weekend. Widely anticipated by locals, the event was to pass into legend. Tens of thousands of people descended on Mullingar, not all of whom were interested in Irish culture. The streets were packed and Gardaí had to baton charge drunken youths who threw bottles at them. The following week local newspapers were full of fierce denunciations of what had occurred. It was the weekend in which the 'swinging sixties' reached Ireland and the occasion would later be immortalised in verse by the poet John Montague in his poem 'The Siege of Mullingar'.

The weekend of the Fleadh coincided with the death of Pope John XXIII and the changes that he had initiated at the second Vatican Council were soon being felt in Mullingar parish; the first Mass entirely in English took place in the cathedral on 29 December 1964.

The assassination of President Kennedy in November 1963 caused widespread shock in

9th Regiment FCA leading the St Patrick's Day Parade in 1994.

Mount Street in the 1950s. Comhaltas Ceoltóirí Éireann was founded in the Midland Hotel on the left-hand side of the street.

The funeral of Cardinal John Glennon in March 1946.

Pearse Street in the 1950s

Moynihan's Shop and the Central Hotel in the 1950s.

Mullingar. Special Masses were held in the cathedral, flags on the County Buildings, courthouse and barracks flew at half-mast and local sporting events were cancelled.

A town with both a river and a canal and close proximity to two lakes, Mullingar suffered flooding problems from time to time and parts of the main street were seriously flooded in November 1965 when the River Brosna burst its banks. But, throughout the fifties and sixties, drainage schemes eliminated some of the marshy areas around the town, freeing up land for commercial development and houses. When Westmeath Motors Garage opened in 1967, it was built on what had been a pond. Council workers had to remove fish from the pond before it could be drained. Drainage works also removed a famous pond near the army barracks known as 'The Lord's Hole', on which the soldiers had skated in wintertime. Legend was that the pond had been bottomless.

In 1966, Mullingar celebrated the fiftieth anniversary of the Easter Rising. A Military Parade was held through the town, memorials were erected at the barracks and the Market House, the schools staged pageants and a new stand was built at Cusack Park.

July 1969 saw some 5,000 people come to Mullingar for the funeral of two IRA members, Peter Barnes and James McCormack, who had been executed in Britain in 1940 for the bomb attack in Coventry in which five people died. IRA men, young and old, virtually took over Mullingar as Mass was held in the cathedral for the two, whose remains had been repatriated by the British Government. McCormack had lived in Mullingar and he and his companion were buried in Ballyglass cemetery, with veteran Belfast IRA member Jimmy Steele giving a speech that signalled the forthcoming split in the IRA. Within weeks, the northern Troubles had begun and within months, the Provisional IRA, conceived in Mullingar, was born.

A 1962 reunion of Mullingar people who had worked in Canada.

As the seventies began, the town's population climbed to around 7,000. While the decade would bring some periods of recession, it was generally a good time for Mullingar. By 1977, an industrial estate had opened and tennis balls were among the items 'made in Mullingar'. Mullingar's first self-service supermarket, McHugh's, had opened in 1963 and more supermarkets followed in the seventies. It was the era of the showbands and of disco, and Mullingar people could see and hear their favourite stars in venues such as the Lake County Hotel, the Horizon Ballroom, the County Hall and Larry Caffrey's singing lounge. Mullingar man Joe Dolan was putting the town on the national and international stage, and two more local men, Tommy and Jimmy Swarbrigg, represented Ireland in the Eurovision.

The Northern conflict cast a shadow over the country throughout the seventies. Most Mullingar people repudiated the IRA's campaign of violence, but there was sympathy for the Nationalist cause. In 1969 and throughout the early 1970s, Catholic children from Belfast were brought to Mullingar for holidays. They were cared for by Civil Defence, the Red Cross and religious orders. Following Bloody Sunday, a protest rally was held in Mullingar and a prominent local Sinn Féin member burned the Union Jack in the Market Square.

In 1971, Mullingar got a new paper with the launch of *The Topic*. It was the *Westmeath Examiner* however, that got a major scoop in October 1976, when the paper reported on the intemperate speech made by the then Minister for Defence, Paddy Donegan, at the opening of a new cook house at the military barracks, in which he called the President, Cearbhall Ó Dálaigh, 'a thundering disgrace'. The *Examiner* report triggered a major political crisis and the President's resignation. The cook house became known as 'Donegan's Downfall'.

The 1980s were a difficult time for Mullingar as the economy sagged and high levels of

Left: An Emigrants' Dance at a time when emigration from Mullingar was very heavy.

Below: Mullingar men working at Port Radium, Canada in the 1950s.

emigration returned. Mullingar was more fortunate than most towns in that most of the established factories either survived or were replaced. Indeed Mullingar's population continued to grow throughout the decade, reaching 12,000 by 1991. New schools opened to cater for the population growth and a new Roman Catholic church also opened, in 1987.

Soldiers from the barracks continued to deploy abroad on UN Missions throughout the seventies and eighties. The most important posting was Lebanon, where Mullingar soldiers served for a period of almost a quarter of a century. The connection between Mullingar and Lebanon would be recognised in 2003 when Mullingar hosted Team Lebanon during the Special Olympics.

As the twentieth century drew to a close, soldiers and Gardaí from the town would also perform peacekeeping duties in Bosnia, Kosovo, Namibia, Macedonia and Eritrea, as well as Liberia and Sierra Leone. By the 1990s, women were serving in the ranks of the Army and FCA in Mullingar for the first time.

The Royal Canal, once a vital part of Mullingar's economic life, had fallen into serious decline during the twentieth century. Children swam in it before the opening of the swimming pool, but it became choked with weeds. The last passenger boat went through Mullingar in 1955 and the canal was closed in 1961, but a local branch of the Royal Canal Amenity Group worked hard to save the canal and gradually restoration began. As a result of their work it was possible, by 1990, to sail as far as Mullingar from Dublin. In August 1999, boats travelled through Mullingar for the first time in thirty years, providing Mullingar once again with a major tourist and local amenity.

Mullingar also acquired other fine amenities in the last decades of the century, including a town park and a swimming pool. Local environmental activists also saved Lough Ennell, one of Mullingar's most beautiful hinterland amenities, from death through pollution.

The role of women was changing in Mullingar, as elsewhere, in the final decades of the century. There were fewer nuns and fewer shopkeepers, but more lawyers, doctors and lay teachers, as well as Gardaí. In 1992, the Revd Sheila Zeitsmann made history when she was ordained to the Church of Ireland Ministry in All Saints church. She thus became the first female priest in the 800 years history of Mullingar Parish. In 1994, Betty Doran became the first female Cathaoirleach of Mullingar Town Commission in its 140 year history and, in 1998, Westmeath became the first county in the Republic of Ireland to have a female County Manager.

By 1996, Mullingar's population had reached 15,000 and the town was expanding rapidly. New housing estates – some with populations as large as the whole of Mullingar a century earlier – began to encircle the town. There were new schools and hotels and more business parks. The 'Celtic Tiger' brought new prosperity and Mullingar became a popular commuter town for Dublin. Traffic congestion increased and there was much relief when the first stage of a bypass opened in 1994 (this bypass was largely completed by 2006).

The Northern Troubles continued to overshadow Ireland throughout the eighties and nineties. Events such as the Enniskillen Bombing in 1987, the Warrington Bombing in 1993 and the Omagh Massacre in 1998, brought Mullingar people out on the streets to sign books of condolence and to hold peace vigils and prayer meetings. Many soldiers from Mullingar spent time on duty patrolling near the border.

By the end of the twentieth century, Mullingar was becoming a more diverse place.

Immigrants from all over the world began to arrive in what was now a prosperous town. People from Poland, Lithuania, Ukraine, Romania, Nigeria, South Africa, Ethiopia, Eritrea, Pakistan, China, Sri Lanka, Burma, Australia, the USA, Brazil, Kurdistan, Tunisia and many other lands made their home in Mullingar. By the early 2000s, up to sixty languages were being spoken in the town. It was a dramatic change in the town's demographic profile. There had long been Italian cafés and Chinese and Indian takeaways in Mullingar. Now Polish and Lithuanian and African food shops and a Halal store appeared as well. It was a rather appropriate development given that Mullingar had actually been founded by immigrants.

On 31 December 1999, hundreds of Mullingar people turned out on a wet evening to say farewell to the old century. A 'Last Light' ceremony took place outside the County Buildings. A few hours later, crowds gathered at the cathedral to welcome in the new millennium. It was a time to reflect on how much had changed in Mullingar over one hundred years and to anticipate what more changes the new century would bring.

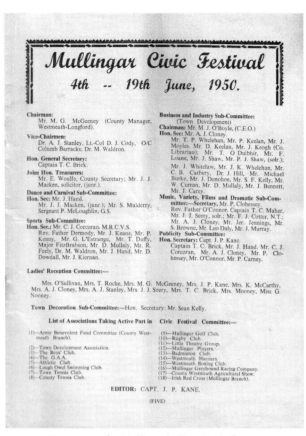

Programme for Mullingar's Civic Festival, 1950.

Party in the Greville Arms to celebrate the victory of 'Quare Times'. The owner of the horse, Cecily Wellman, is seated second from the left.

The Dream of Gerontius, performed in the cathedral in 1958.

Lt.-Gen. HARBAKHSH SINGH (right), G.O.C.-in-C. Western Command, receives Lt.-Gen. Bakhtiar Rana of Pakistan at U.N. Headquarters, Amritsar. The meeting, for the withdrawal of armed personnel on either side, was presided over by Brig.-Gen. Tulio Marambio (extreme left), representative of the U.N. Secretary-General.

Colonel M.J. O'Donnell in Kashmir.

Appeal for Congo
Christmas Fund, 1960.

38th Infantry Battalion Heavy Mortar Troop, who served in the Congo from October 1962 to April 1963.

Back row, from left to right: Gnr J. Doherty, Gnr T. Irwin, Cpl T. Gavin, Gnr D. Watters, Gnr P. Connolly, Gnr J. Geoghegan, Gnr P. Devaney, Cpl J. Quirke, Gnr P. McCann, Gnr J. Rooney, Cpl Wallen, Cpl P. Nea.

Third row: Gnr T. McCrann, Gnr L. Ainsworth, Gnr L. O'Keeffe, Gnr P. Cathy, Gnr B. Grealish, Gnr P. Kelly, Gnr K. Prendergast, Gnr P.J. Dunne, Sgt O. Walsh, Gnr M. Prendergast, Sgt K. Skeehan.

Second row: Gnr T. Clarke, Gnr P. Whelan, Gnr D. Kennedy. Gnr C. McNamee, Gnr J. Murphy, Gnr P. Hughes, Gnr M. Dowd, Gnr T. Flanagan, Gnr J. Joyce, Gnr V. Harte.

First row: Sgt P. Brennan, B/S.A. Byrne, Lt L. Hughes, Capt. T. O'Boyle, Lt-Col. M. Harrington, Lt W. O'Dwyer, Sgt J. Byrne, Sgt D. Crone.

A circus elephant crossing Dominick Street in 1960.

An Insight — Exclusively for
You — Into the Future

TAILTEANN
TEXTILES LTD.

PROUDLY PRESENT A SMALL
SELECTION FROM THEIR

Spring/Summer 1966
Range

LATEST STYLING IN FULL FASHIONED KNITWEAR
FOR LADIES AND GENTLEMEN

•

WONDERFUL SELECTION OF THE SO POPULAR
SWEATER DRESSES IN LAMBSWOOL, LAMBS-
WOOL/ANGORA AND CAMEL HAIR
STYLINGS TO SUIT ALL AGES FROM THE LATEST
'OP-ART" GEOMETRICS FOR THE TEENAGERS TO
THE ELEGANT FASHIONS SUITED TO THE MORE
MATURE LADY

IN THE SHOPS EARLY NEXT YEAR

Be Irish & Buy Tailteann

Tailteann Textiles was one of Mullingar's first factories

Crown Prince Carl Gustav of Sweden fishing on Lough Ennel with Dr Billy Waldron in 1964.

Medical staff with a helicopter at the County Hospital in the 1960s.

Rex Beaumont, the last private owner of Belvedere House.

Sean Lemass, then Taoiseach, in Mullingar with town band during the 1965 General Election.

President De Valera at the Consecration of Bishop William Dunne in 1964.

The Lido Café and staff in the 1960s.

Members of the Mullingar ICA in 1977.

Council workers Ned Hynes and Ker Willis, 1960s.

A military parade in Dominick Street in 1966 to mark the Golden Jubilee of the Easter Rising.

Sinn Féin TD Rory O'Brady, second from right, following his election as Longford–Westmeath TD, 1957.

The funeral of IRA hunger striker Michael Gaughan passes through Mullingar in June 1974.

I NDIL CHUIMHNE
CAPT. COMPLACHTA PEADAR O BEARAIN agus CAPT. FOIRNE SEAMUS Mac CORMAIC
A CUIREADH CHUN BAIS I BPRIOSUIN WINSON GREEN, I SASAIN
AR AN 7TH FEABHRA 1940
GUR SAIBHRE FLAITHEAS DE A N-ANAMNACHA.

The Republican plot at Ballyglass containing the graves of IRA members Peter Barnes and James McCormick.

Miss Westmeath Competition in the early 1970s.

Wren Boys in Mullingar, 1960s.

Young ballet dancers in the 1960s.

Horslips and local teenagers in the County Hall, 1970s.

Dancers from the French Town of Molsheim, which was twinned with Mullingar in the early 1990s.

Dr Garret Fitzgerald at a Fine Gael Convention in the Bloomfield Hotel, 1986.

Mullingar army personnel leaving for a tour of Duty with the 84th Battalion in Lebanon.
Standing, from left to right: Gnr Peter Scally, Gnr Darren Greene, Cpl Des Curley, Cpl Joe Boyce, Sgt Willie Reilly, Gnr Andrew Flynn, Gnr Greg Cleary.
Seated: Gnr David Quinn, Gnr William Bastic, Gnr Paul Connolly, Gnr Eamonn O'Malley, Lt-Col Ray Twomey, Gnr Damien Greene, Gnr Graham, Pte Liam Smith, Sgt Joe Quinn.

Mullingar men on peacekeeping duty in Bosnia, June 2000.

A rally to celebrate the reopening of the Royal Canal through Mullingar in 1999.

Albert Reynolds opens the Mullingar bypass.

Peace rally in Mullingar in the aftermath of the Warrington bombing.

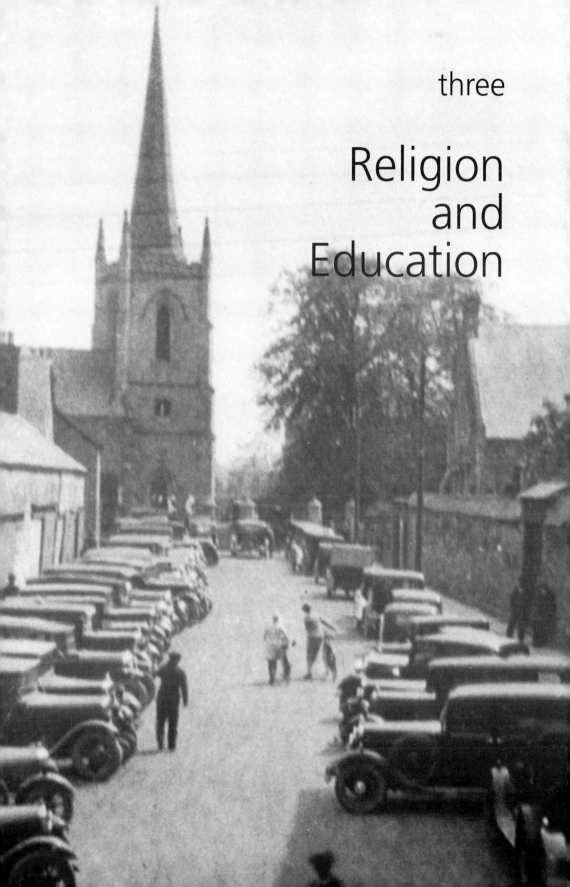

three

Religion
and
Education

Throughout the twentieth century, Mullingar's faith communities played an important part in the life of the town. One particularly important area in which they played a significant role was that of education. The vast majority of Mullingar people received at least part of their education in schools run by religious orders and denominations.

At the start of the twentieth century, Mullingar, like most Irish towns outside Ulster, was overwhelmingly Roman Catholic, with Catholics making up more than 85 per cent of the population. There were, however, a significant number of Protestants. The main Protestant denominations were Church of Ireland (Anglican), Presbyterian and Methodist. According to the 1911 Census, Mullingar had 4,561 Roman Catholics, 890 Church of Ireland, 45 Methodists, 37 Presbyterians and 6 from all other dominations (including 2 Jews).

Mullingar formally became a cathedral town in 1830 when the Roman Catholic Bishop John Cantwell moved his residence to Mullingar from Navan. Cathedral House, designed by the noted Irish Architect William Hague, had been built as a residence for Bishop Thomas Nulty in 1880 and was known as the Bishop's Palace.

At the start of the twentieth century Mullingar's cathedral was known as St Mary's church. It was 'The first substantial post reformation Catholic church' in Mullingar. It was built in 1836 and stood on the site now occupied by the Cathedral of Christ the King. It was a fine building, but, as early as 1900, the Church authorities were setting their sights on building something larger. Bishop Gaffney announced that fundraising would begin to provide Mullingar with a new cathedral, 'one worthy of the large and historic diocese of Meath'.

The then enormous sum of £15,000 was immediately subscribed and the newly appointed Archbishop of St Louis, Dr John Glennon, who had attended the neighbouring CBS school as a boy, preached in the cathedral in 1903, appealing for funds.

Bishop Gaffney did not live to see the cathedral become a reality, however, nor did his successor, Dr Laurence Gaughran, who had the difficult task of steering Mullingar Parish and Meath Diocese through the traumas of the First World War and the 1916-23 'Troubles'. Political turmoil and hard economic times meant that it was not until the early 1930s that Bishop Thomas Mulvany was in a position to sign the contracts allowing work on the new cathedral to begin.

The architect chosen was Ralph Byrne of Dublin and the building cost £199,500. Bishop Mulvany cut the first sod at a ceremony on 31 March 1932. On 6 August 1933, the cornerstone was laid and the sermon was preached by the indefatigable fundraiser Archbishop Glennon. On the historic day of 6 July 1936, Mass was said for the final time in the old cathedral and for the first time in the new one.

On 6 September 1936, the new cathedral was formally dedicated to Christ the King in a ceremony attended by Cardinal McRory of Armagh, the Papal Nuncio and twelve Irish Bishops, as well as Eamon De Valera and twelve members of the government. Dr Glennon was the preacher and his powerful sermon included sharp comments on the pretensions of Hitler, Mussolini, Stalin and the other totalitarian leaders then polluting the world.

The formal consecration of the cathedral took place on 30 August 1939. Four days later, on Sunday 3 September 1939, Mass was celebrated to mark the occasion, attended by Cardinal McRory, ten Bishops and the Lord Abbots of Roscrea and Mount Melleray. It was a momentous day in world history – the day on which the Second World War began. But in Mullingar, it was a day of great joy and celebration with flags and bunting everywhere. The only impact made by the war on the celebrations was that due to orders for blackout, plans to have the cathedral floodlit had to be abandoned. On the Saturday and Sunday nights, like the rest of the town and country, it was in darkness.

Since 1936, the Cathedral of Christ the King has been Mullingar's landmark building – its twin towers and dome dominating the horizon all across the town. The artwork inside and outside the cathedral is of very fine quality. Among those who contributed to the artwork were Albert Power RHA, William Earley, Fr Aengus Buckley and Henry Thompson. Possibly the most noteworthy and historic artworks in the building are two mosaics by the distinguished Russian artist Boris Anrep. The first of these, depicting the lighting of the first paschal fire in Ireland by St Patrick, was done in 1948. Most of the work was done in Anrep's Paris studio and then completed in the cathedral. Interestingly, one of the first people to see the St Patrick mosaic in place was the then British Prime Minister, Clement Attlee, who was holidaying in Westmeath and was brought by a friend to visit the cathedral. A second mosaic, depicting the presentation of Mary in the temple, was commissioned by Bishop John Kyne for the Marian Year Celebrations in 1954. Of particular important historical note is the face of St Anne in this mosaic, said to be modelled on the face of the great Russian poet Anna Akhmatova, who was once Boris Anrep's lover.

Both old and new cathedrals have witnessed historic events in the story of twentieth-century Mullingar. In the early years of the century, Roman Catholic soldiers in the army garrisons attended Mass there and members of the famous Connaught Rangers Regiment attended church wearing shamrock for the St Patrick's Day religious ceremonies. In September 1922, hundreds attended Requiem Mass for the souls of Michael Collins and Arthur Griffith. In March 1946, three Cardinals, numerous Bishops and priests and hundreds of townspeople were present for the funeral Mass of Cardinal Glennon.

In September 1989, big celebrations were held to mark the golden jubilee of the cathedral's consecration. During the 1990s, extensive renovation work was carried out on the roof and the organ gallery, and the restored building was fully reopened in November 1997. In May 1998, President Mary McAleese visited the cathedral's award-winning museum. The cathedral was also the focus for the celebrations welcoming in the Jubilee Year 2000 and the new millenium and century on 1 January 2000.

Most of the twentieth-century Bishops of Meath, all of whom were consecrated in Mullingar, are buried in the cathedral grounds, with the exception of the man whose idea it was to build the new cathedral, Bishop Gaffney, and Cardinal John D'Alton.

On the outskirts of Mullingar stand a number of other Roman Catholic churches, most of which were in existence before the start of the twentieth century. Gainstown and Brotenstown go back in origin to the eighteenth century, although both were renovated extensively during the twentieth century – Brotenstown in 1976-79 and Gainstown in 1954. The church at Walshestown is the oldest in the parish of Mullingar. It too was renovated in the twentieth century. This church has now acquired a new historic significance relating to the entertainment history of Mullingar; the singer Joe Dolan, one of Mullingar's most popular and nationally known figures, is buried there.

As Mullingar town grew during the twentieth century, new Roman Catholic churches and chapels opened to cater for the population. In 1987, St Paul's church was opened on the Delvin Road.

REV Fr KELLY REV Fr WOODS REV Fr DALY REV Fr POLAND REV Fr MAGEE

Mullingar parish clergy in the early 1900s.

St Mary's CBS and the old cathedral, c.1900.

St Paul's was the first church to reflect the rules of Vatican Two Council concerning the celebrant facing the congregation and was built in a quite different style to the ultramontane triumphalism of the Cathedral of Christ the King. The army barracks chapel was consecrated as a Roman Catholic church in the 1920s and, in 1968, the opening of the Sacred Heart Private Hospital by Franciscan nuns provided another place of worship.

A large number of Catholic Associations were set up in the nineteenth and twentieth centuries to cater for the spiritual needs of Mullingar's Roman Catholic community. Concerns about the abuse of alcohol led to the founding of St Mary's Temperance Society in 1895 by a Christian Brother, Hugh Hurley. The society was open to all men over twenty-one and women were admitted in 1906. The society ran a highly successful dramatic class and held a Temperance Bail in the Market House. They had a club house with a reading room and billiards room which was situated in Church Lane. Members of the society were expected to attend Mass and receive communion and they wore a society ribbon and medal. The society, which had support from the clergy and bishop, survived until 1935.

Support for temperance also led to the founding in Mullingar of a branch of the Pioneer Total Abstinence Association on 22 January 1924. The first President was Michael Daly and the first Secretary was Loreto Killian, with Thomas Coleman as Treasurer.

Confraternities and sodalities for men and women have existed in Mullingar Parish since the 1860s, with confraternity of the Holy Family dating back to 1867. On the occasion of the Diamond Jubilee celebrations in May 1927, there was a procession of the Blessed Sacrament through the main streets.

This inaugurated the Corpus Christi procession, which, for most of the rest of the twentieth century, was one of the biggest religious events held in the town, involving hundreds of people, including the schools and even the army. The centenary celebrations of the confraternity in 1967 were marked with special ceremonies in the cathedral.

For women there were two important sodalities; the Association of the Sacred Heart of Jesus was founded in 1896 and the sodality of Our Lady, better known as the Children of Mary, was formed in 1878. Both sodalities organised annual retreats for members and were involved in charitable works. The confraternity and sodality banners, carried through the town on occasions such as the Corpus Christi procession, are displayed in the cathedral museum.

The Legion of Mary set up a presidium in Mullingar on 27 November 1932 with the encouragement of Bishop Mulvany. The first President was Kitty Coffey, with Maria Hetherson as Vice President. The first Secretary was Kitty Delaney and the Spiritual Director was Fr John McKeever, whose top hat is now in the museum. Presidia for men and for children were formed later. The Legion originally met in a building known as the Penny Dinner Depot or the Legion Rooms. Sadly this building was destroyed by fire in 1962 and most of the records destroyed.

The Apostolic Work Society was founded in 1921 by Fr E. Crinion and its annual exhibition of its work for the missions, which was held on Mission Sunday, became one of the highlights of the Mullingar parish year.

Other associations include the Knights of Columbanus, established in 1930, whose founding members included the distinguished medical practitioner, author and actor, Dr Tony Stanley; the St Joseph's Young Priests' Society, founded in 1921 and the Ecumenical St Dominick's

Interior of the old cathedral.

Community Centre, which opened in 1970.

Throughout the twentieth century, the cathedral choirs of Mullingar made a major contribution to the musical life of the church and the town. Evelyn Dore was one of the most significant figures in this musical history. She and her husband Philip came to Mullingar in 1938 when Philip was appointed as organist in the new cathedral. When he left town in the early 1940s, she succeeded him and directed the choir for forty years, setting the highest standards.

All Saints church has been a site for religious worship for 800 years. Since 1560 it has been the parish church of the Church of Ireland community. Over the course of the twentieth century, that community would decline in numbers but remain at the heart of town life.

In the early 1900s, the Church of Ireland membership included local gentry, such as Lord Greville (landlord of Mullingar and Chairman of the County Council), Charles Brinsley Marley of Belvedere, and the County Secretary C. Levinge. The business and professional classes of Mullingar were also well represented, and there were also numbers of soldiers and policemen.

From 1893 until 1926, the Rector of Mullingar was Dr Robert Seymour. He was helped in his work of running the parish by elected churchwardens, glebe wardens and a select vestry of twelve men chosen each Easter to run the finances and business of the parish for the coming year. In 1914, the select vestrymen were E. Loftus, J.C. Bannon, T. Hill, J. Gibbons, F.J. Farrell, C.V. Porter, F. Mitchell, T.G. Thorpe, A. Kerrison and J. Speer.

As well as All Saints, Church of Ireland services were held at the army barracks and at the asylum. Outlying parish churches which would be absorbed into the Mullingar union of parishes during the twentieth century included Moyliskar, Portanshangan

The Procession to Solemn Pontifical High Mass on the occasion of laying the Foundation Stone of the Cathedral on August 6th, 1933.

Procession of clergy at the laying of the cathedral foundation stone in August 1933.

and Enniscoffey.

The Parochial Hall beside All Saints had opened in 1888. It served not just the Church of Ireland community but the whole town. It was a venue for concerts, plays, jumble sales and pet shows. In the 1910s the hall was being hired out at a rate of 2s 6d per night or 10s a week.

In December 1925, Dr Seymour retired and was replaced in April 1926 by Revd George Berry, whose incumbency was also very long. He stayed in Mullingar until 1958. When he arrived in Mullingar the select vestry comprised: W.E. Bourke, B. Watson, A.E. Mason, W.J. Graham, C. Porter, J. Winckworth, J.E. Tyrrell, A. Campbell, J. Halliwell and R. Ramesy. In 1932, a fundraising committee raised £120 to help pay for the installation of electric light in the church.

The Church of Ireland population declined after the end of British rule and emigration further reduced numbers. For many decades the community, while very well integrated into the life of the town and loyal to the new state, retained a sense of affinity with the British Commonwealth of Nations. Remembrance Sunday was observed annually and collections taken up for the Earl Haig Poppy Appeal. Members of the congregation served in both world wars and some did not return from these conflicts. In 1952, a service was held to give thanks for the life of King George VI. But Revd Berry also took part in the religious services held during 'Brigade Week' in Mullingar in 1942 and reminded the congregation of the need to recognise and serve the Irish State.

In 1958, Ian MacDougall from Co. Cavan became Rector. He was extremely popular and was at the forefront of efforts to bring the Churches of Mullingar closer together. In October 1972, a landmark religious service took place in All Saints church with the holding of an Ecumenical Harvest Festival Service addressed by leading Roman Catholic theologian, Fr Michael Hurley.

Members of the Presentation Convent school choir in 1933.

The service was also attended by the Church of Ireland Bishop of Meath and Kildare, Dr R. Pike. Fr Hurley had also addressed the first ecumenical meeting in the town in 1966.

Revd McDougall enjoyed good relations with the Roman Catholic clergy in the town. In December 1966, he attended the funeral of Bishop Kyne and the select vestry passed a unanimous vote of sympathy to the Catholic community on the death of the Bishop.

In 1962, vestry members included T.L. Hutchinson, R.F. Taylor, T.S. Mitchell, Colonel Howard-Bury, W.E. Bourke, N. Clarke, W.T. Rolston, J. Fitzpatrick, N.C. Fletcher, W. Godwin, Dr G. Jackson, G. Bell, N. Carr, J. Minion and T.E. Winckworth. By now women could serve on select vestries and Mrs McCall was the one female member.

As with the Roman Catholic community, the Church of Ireland parishioners had a number of associations to help extend spiritual activities beyond Sunday morning church services. These included the Boys' Brigade and the Girls' Friendly Society. The Friendly Society held annual jumble sales to help raise funds for GFS Missionary activities. In November 1951, for example, the jumble sale raised £53. There was also a youth club. Many women belonged to the Mothers' Union. In the early part of the century, many parishioners were involved in running the Westmeath Protestant Orphans' Society. This society, founded in 1840, took care of 'children whose parents [or breadwinning parent] had died'. In the days before social welfare this was often vital work. Children were cared for in their own homes by nurses appointed by the society. When old enough, the children were sent to boarding schools or apprenticed to Protestant employers. The society's work helped keep children out of the workhouse.

A children's Temperance Society was founded in 1900 and lasted until the 1930s. In 1984, Revd Fred Gilmore came to Mullingar. He had a curate from 1989, the first time since 1918

Cathedral

OF

Christ the King,

Mullingar

Dedication Souvenir.

Mullingar, Sunday, 6th September, 1936

PRICE --- SIXPENCE

PRINTED AND PUBLISHED BY JOHN P. HAYDEN, AT "WESTMEATH EXAMINER" PRINTING WORKS,
MULLINGAR.

Booklet for the cathedral's dedication cermony.

that All Saints had two clergy. In 1992, Revd Sheila Zeitzmann became curate, just two years after the Church of Ireland first ordained women to the priesthood.

In 1994, Revd Patrick Carmody became Rector. During his tenure, the Parochial Hall was sold and extensive renovations were carried out on the interior of the church. In 2002, a special service and exhibition was held to mark the 800th anniversary of the first mention of All Saints Church.

The Presbyterian community in Mullingar dates back at least 200 years and the church was opened in 1824. At the start of the century, the congregation numbered just under forty.

Bob Eivers, who worked on the building of the cathedral, pictured in 1936.

The St Anne's chapel mosaic in the cathedral, created by Boris Anrep in 1954.

Numbers tended to go up and down depending on which British regiments were in town, with the congregation increasing when Scottish soldiers were in the barracks. Mullingar was part of the presbytery of Athlone and the Minister served mission stations in Kilbeggan and Tyrrellspass. At the start of the twentieth century, the Minister was William Cupples McCullough. His son later became a famous broadcaster on BBC Radio as a presenter of *Children's Hour*, where he was known as 'Uncle Mac'. From 1905 to 1913, the Minister was Robert Steele Coffee. There was then a vacancy until Revd Martin Rea was called to Mullingar in 1915. By then there were just twenty-three communicant members of the congregation. It was Revd Rea who guided his congregation through the difficult transition from being part of the United Kingdom to being a minority within a minority in an independent state that defined itself as Gaelic and Catholic. The departure of British troops and the RIC further reduced the congregation to fifteen communicants by 1928. A number of short incumbencies followed through the 1930s until the appointment of Revd J.H. Black in 1938, who ministered in Mullingar until his retirement in 1960. He was the last Minister to live in the manse, built in 1863, beside the church in Castle Street. The Revd Black's family owned a large tortoise, which was often seen wandering around the church grounds!

In 1960, Revd Black retired and the manse was sold. For the rest of the century, Mullingar was linked with Kells and Corboy, Co. Longford and Ministers did not live in Mullingar. In 1971, Mrs Susan Graham was ordained as the first female Elder in Mullingar Presbyterian history.

A new era for Mullingar's Presbyterian community began in the early 2000s when Revd Stephen Lockington became the first resident Minister in Mullingar for forty years. In the latter years of the twentieth century, the congregation had dwindled to fewer than a dozen. But as the new millennium began numbers dramatically increased to the highest in the congregation's history.

In 1965, a chapter in Mullingar's spiritual history came to an end, when the Methodist meeting house closed after 160 years. The Methodists had first come to Mullingar in the eighteenth century and their chapel (or meeting house) had opened in 1806. At the beginning of the 1900s the Minister was Revd John Carson and the congregation numbered seventy-five.

As with the Presbyterians, numbers tended to fluctuate depending on which British regiment was in town, with numbers increasing when soldiers from Methodist strongholds such as the north of England or Wales were around. Apart from the military and police, Mullingar's Methodists were mostly drawn from the business or professional class.

After 1922, with the departure of the British, the numbers of Methodists dwindled. Mullingar was part of the Tullamore circuit and the Minister came over from there to take the service every Sunday at 9a.m. The last Minister was Revd A. Bradshaw.

As the twentieth century drew to a close, the religious diversity of Mullingar was growing. Jehovah Witnesses built themselves a Witness Hall on the eastern outskirts of the town in the 1980s, and a Mormon presence was established in the 1990s.

African immigrants introduced Pentecostalism and a number of Evangelical churches also opened. At the start of the twentieth century there were two Jews living in Mullingar and there were the same number one hundred years later. In 1901, no Muslims lived in Mullingar. By 2006, there would be 242 and Mullingar would have a Mosque.

President McAleese visiting the cathedral museum in May 1998.

Bishop John Kyne arriving in Mullingar in July 1947.

The funeral of Bishop John Kyne in December 1966.

The funeral of Bishop John McCormack in September 1996.

This remarkable picture shows Bishop John Kyne's arrival in Mullingar on 11 July 1947.

Cathedral stewards at the consecration of Bishop Dunne in 1964.
Back row, left to right: Bobby Bradley, Jack Creamer, Jack McCoy, Joe Gerrity, John Reilly, Matt Purcell, James Savage, Paddy Keogh, Tom Healy, Tom Coffey.
Second row: Declan Quigley, Chris McEnroe, Jack Reynolds, Jim Ryan, Paddy Code, Peter Kenny, Luke McAuley, Vincent Brophy, Jack Murtagh, Raymond Carr, Pat McCormack, Jim Dalton, John Lyons, Seamus Murphy, George Mitchell, Phil Mullally, James McDonnell, Richard Cummins.
Front row: Joe Brennan, William Thorogood, Peter Kenny, Brother McGrath, Revd Coleman, Revd Joseph Dermody, Paddy Price, Frank Killeen, Revd John McCormack.

Missions' sale of work, Parish Community Centre, 1999.

This building once housed the Mullingar National Workingmen's Club and the Temperance Club.

Mullingar Pioneers at centenary celebrations in Dublin, 1999.

Members of the Holy Family Confraternity, 1920s.

Children of Mary with their veils and blue cloaks carrying a beautifully decorated statue of Our Lady at a May procession in the Convent grounds.

Children of Mary procession in Presentation Convent grounds.

Mullingar Legion of Mary Members at Knock.

Girls' Club Christmas Party c.1970.
From left to right: Carmel English, Hanna O'Hara, Frances Maher, Sister Joseph Christine Smyth, Una Daly, Revd J. Conway, Marian Lynch, Bishop McCormick, M. Rock, Sr Maureen Waldron, T. Lacey, Carmel O'Keeffe, Una O'Leary, Brigid Spellman, Nora McNamee, Nancy Fagan.

Mrs Evelyn Dore conducting the cathedral choir.

All Saints church in the early 1900s.

Harvest Thanksgiving Service in All Saints church, October 1972.

President Mary Robinson with Revd Fred Gilmor, Rector of Mullingar, and Revd Sheila Zeitsmann (Curate).

The ordination of Revd Sheila Zeitsmann in All Saints church.

Bishop Richard Clarke at the 800th anniversary celebrations of All Saints church.

The former Methodist Meeting House.

The building of the Jehovah's Witnesses Kingdom Hall,
completed in just two days, in 1986.

Presentation Sisters with Revd E. O'Reilly in 1898.

EDUCATION

When the twentieth century began, Mullingar had three primary schools and two secondary schools. The oldest was Presentation Convent, established in 1826. St Mary's Christian Brothers School was almost half a century old in 1900, and the newest school was Loreto Convent, which opened its doors as Mullingar's first secondary school for girls in 1881. The Protestant community in Mullingar was served by the Church of Ireland National School which, at that time, was in Harbour Street. The twentieth century saw all these schools expand. In the case of Presentation, major extensions were built in 1921, 1935 and 1936. The cost of the renovations in the 1930s was £11,600. In the early years of the century there were three classrooms, referred to by the pupils as 'the gallery, the deskus and t'other room'.

By the 1950s, a growing population meant that Presentation School now had more pupils and further expansion was necessary. It was decided to split the school into junior and senior sections and a new Senior School was built in Harbour Street. The new building, Scoil na Maighdine Muire, opened in 1957. Further extensions took place in the 1960s and 1970s to both junior and senior schools. St Mary's CBS (also known as The Heavey Institute in honour of the man whose money set up the school) had opened in 1856. It was both a national and secondary school by 1900 and had about 600 pupils.

By the 1950s, the numbers of pupils had grown and the original building could not cope. A large-scale fundraising drive began in 1954 to build a new national school. The fundraising was spearheaded by Bishop John Kyne and by the past pupils' union, headed by Dr Stanley. Following the major celebrations of the school's centenary in 1956, work began on the new building and it was opened in October 1959 by the Minister for Education, Dr Patrick Hillery. The cost of the building was £50,653. For some years during the 1960s it was featured on RTÉ during the nightly playing of the National Anthem. Meanwhile, the original school building was renovated and by 1962 it accommodated 145 pupils. However, the introduction of free secondary education in the mid 1960s led to a big increase in secondary school numbers and a new secondary school was opened in 1972. In 1980, a new gymnasium opened which has since served not just the school but the wider community, as it has been used as a concert venue and as an election count centre. Famous past pupils include singer Joe Dolan, Cardinal Archbishop John Glennon and the CEO of Ryanair, Michael O'Leary. By the end of the century, the school was flourishing, but the number of Christian Brothers – once the majority among the staff – had dwindled and, in 2006, the last Brothers left Mullingar after 150 years.

Loreto Convent opened in 1881. Originally it was intended to be a Mercy convent as the money for the foundation came from a Mercy Sister, Frances Kerrigan. But then Bishop Nulty changed his mind and brought in Loreto Sisters instead, although Sister Kerrigan continued wearing her own religious habit and following the Mercy Rule.

Loreto was the first girls' secondary school in the town and accommodated boarders as well as day pupils; there were ten boarders in 1900. There was much emphasis on art, music and the domestic skills of cookery and sewing, but the Loreto order has always been a progressive one and the nuns also encouraged their pupils to use their brains and imbued them with self-confidence and a belief that they were as good as boys.

The school soon began to expand, with a junior wing being added in 1925, which lasted until

MULLINGAR MEMORY FROM 1919: How many readers of this paper, looking at a picture taken eighty four years ago at Presentation Convent, would be able to identify some of those in the picture? Believe it or not, every single girl in this picture, taken at the Mullingar school in 1919, was identified for us by a lady who was among those photographed on the occasion, Margaret Caffrey, of Grand Parade, Mullingar, who deserves special thanks. Back row (l. to r.) Bridgie Farrell, Maggie Gavigan, May Cakebread, Jane Doyle, May Attwell, Bridie Mullen, Agnes Carroll, Josie Feeney, Lou Hickey, Kathleen Coen, Kay Gormley. Middle Row (l. to r.) Ita Byrne, Maggie Caffrey, Chrissie Skelly, Rita Coyne, Nora Bracken, Lizzie Wemmes, Molly Owens, Kittie Harte, Claire Sullivan. Front row (l. to r.) Gertie Lane, Annie Devine, Essie Farrell, Mary F. Heavey, Chrissie Keena, Rose A Lennon, Maggie Skelly, Maggie McGrath.

Presentation School pupils, 1919.

Presentation Sisters in 1926.

Presentation Junior School pupils, 1930.

the 1960s. Big extensions were carried out in 1959-60 and a new chapel opened in 1968. In the 1960s a car was bought for the nuns. More extensions took place in 1969 and yet another extension was opened in 1984. The last boarders left the school in 1975. A fire in September 1984 caused extensive damage in the new extension, but fortunately the damage was soon repaired.

As with other religious orders, the numbers of Loreto nuns dwindled in the latter part of the century and by the 1980s the majority of teachers were lay people. From the late 1960s the school began employing male teachers and the first male Principal, Michael Kearns, was appointed in 1996. Famous past pupils include Ada English, Sinn Féin TD and pioneering doctor; Sheila Mullally, fashion designer, and Ailish Tynan, singer.

The first venue for vocational or technical education in Mullingar was actually the old jail, which closed in 1900. Classes in woodwork, needlework and cooking were held, attended by many of the young men and lady workers of the town. As numbers grew, what had been the Governor's House was occupied, and two rooms in the new County Buildings were added after 1913. In 1914, the school rented a typewriter at 7s 6d per month. The curriculum gradually expanded to include first aid, horticulture, shorthand, spinning and engineering. By the late 1920s a commercial school had also been added.

The First World War delayed the building of a technical school until 1920. The Second World War disrupted plans to build a new school, but the Vocational Education Act of 1930 led to the establishment of a Vocational School Committee in Mullingar, and in 1953, Mullingar Vocational School – popularly known as 'the Tech' – opened on a new site at Millmount Road. It soon acquired a very good reputation among employers and, with the Free Education Act, it took began to expand in the 1970s. By the end of the century it had been renamed Mullingar Community College.

In 1908, the diocesan seminary for Meath, St Finians College, was moved from Navan to Mullingar. The building cost was £30,000. The chapel was added in 1913. Many of the boys went on to join the priesthood and several became Bishops. But not all students became priests;

Presentation Sisters in 1958.
From left to right: Sr Gertrude Shortall, Sr DeLourdes Grennan, Sr Dolores (Maureen) Waldron and Sr Rosario Flanagan.

many entered other professions. By the 1980s the school had 253 students. In 1969, *schola cantorium* became one of the most successful schools of music in Ireland.

As the new millennium started, the huge fall in religious vocations prompted the decision to end boarding and open the school to girls.

In the mid-twentieth century, another secondary school existed in Mullingar. In 1933, the Franciscan Sister of the Immaculate Conception opened a pre-novitiate for girls at Bloomfield House near Belvedere on the shores of Lough Ennell. The house was bought from Colonel Howard Bury of Belvedere and the novitiate opened in July 1933. The first superior was Mother Mary Scholastica. Postulants were sent to Rome until the Second World War, after which they stayed on at Bloomfield. Because the postulants were so young, a secondary school was set up for them and in 1963 it opened with sixty pupils. However, by the early 1970s, the school seemed unlikely to grow and in 1977, Bloomfield Convent closed. The remains of the Franciscan Sisters who had died during the forty-year history of the Convent were re-intered in Ballyglass Cemetery.

New primary schools opened in Mullingar in the last decades of the century. St Colman's School opened in 1979 and the town's first Gaelscoil opened in 1994, reflecting a new enthusiasm for the language among many young Mullingar people. In 1984, St Bridget Primary and Secondary Special School opened. The increasing diversity of the town would be reflected in the opening of the first multi-denominational primary school in the town for more than 150 years.

Finally the contribution of religious orders to the medical wellbeing of Mullingar must not be forgotten. In 1898, the Mercy Sisters came to Mullingar to run a hospital at the workhouse.

Four Sisters took up duties caring for some of the poorest and most marginalised sections of Mullingar society at a salary of £30 per year. The Superior was Veronica O'Growney, sister of the distinguished Gaelic language scholar Fr Eugene O'Growney (she was also Head Nurse and Head Gardener).

In 1921, the workhouse was transferred into a county home. St Ann's fever hospital was another part of the complex. In 1936, when the new county hospital opened near the workhouse, the Mercy Sisters worked there as well, with Sister Camillus Lynam as the First Matron and a new convent building, St Brigid's. In the 1950s, the fever hospital became a TB unit as part of the national campaign against the disease. The county home suffered a great deal from lack of funding over the years but much was done under the regime of Matron Sister Kevin from 1959. Over the decades, doctors such as Dillon, Kelly and Keenan also did alot to help raise standards of care.

The Mercy Sisters' involvement with the county home (renamed St Mary's Hospital in 1950) and the County Hospital ended in the 1990s, when the remaining Sisters moved out and lay matrons were appointed.

Above: Presentation Senior School pupils and teachers, 1957/8.

Below: Bishop McCormick and clergy at the Presentation Convent 150th Anniversary Celebrations in 1975.

Centenary celebrations of St Mary's CBS, 27 June 1956.
Lef to right: Peter Kiernan (Past Pupils' Union), Brother Campion (Superior CBS), Bishop John Kyne, Brother Clancy (Superior General), Fr Andrew Shaw.

The opening of CBS Junior School in 1959 by Dr Patrick Hillery.

Confirmation class at St Mary's CBS in 1974.

Loreto Convent in the early 1900s.

Loreto pupils in the early twentieth century.

A. M. D. G.

LORETO CONVENT, MULLINGAR.

(Co. Westmeath)

(FOUNDED 1881)

BOARDING AND DAY SCHOOL.

Under the Patronage of the Most Rev. Dr. Mulvany,
Lord Bishop of Meath.

Pupils prepared for all Public Examinations

SCHOOL RE-OPENS TUESDAY, SEPT. 8th.

For Terms, apply to:

THE SUPERIORESS.

Advertisement for Loreto Convent, 1936.

Loreto Convent Sisters in 1977.
Back row, left to right: Sr Alocoque Fitzpatrick, Sr Martha Mullally, Sr Helen McCarthy, Sr Ita Gorman, Sr Josephine Sinnott, Sr Anna Brady, Sr Dominic Connolly, Sr Josepha Dooley, Sr Imelda Duffy.
Front row: Sr Margaret Murray, Sr Ligouri Sheerin, Sr Philomena Gallagher, Sr Bernadette Kelly, Sr Carmel Collier.

St Finian's College, pictured soon after it opened in 1908.

St Finian's College production of *HMS Pinafore*.

St Finian's College staff, 1960s.

The opening of the novitiate at Bloomfield Convent, 15 August 1963.

Missionary Franciscan Sisters at Bloomfield Convent, c.1965.

Pupils at Mullingar's first Irish language school in 1994.

The Mercy Convent at St Mary's Hospital.

Mercy Nuns and Dr Dillon Kelly at the workhouse hospital.

Staff of St Loman's Hospital with Bishop McCormick in 1970.

Party for Dr Keelan's retirement from the County Hospital in the 1950s.

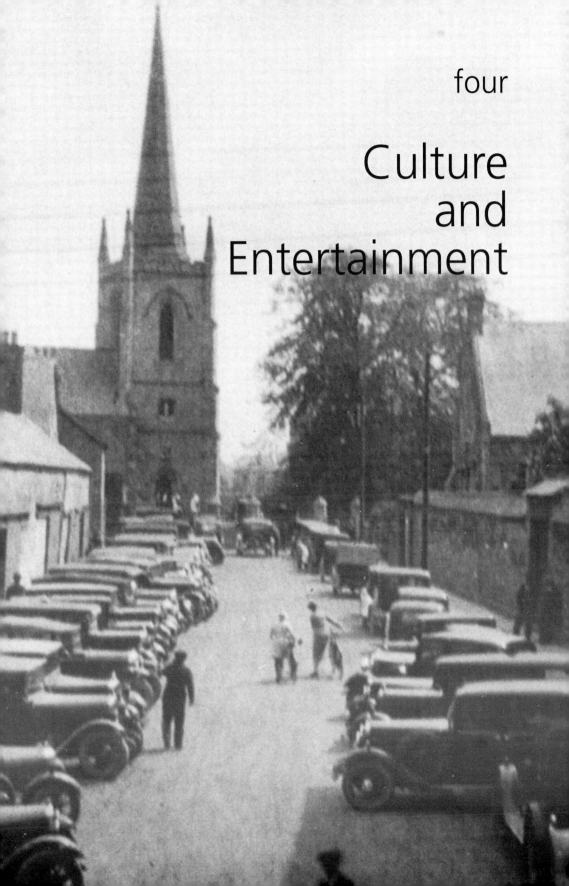

four

Culture
and
Entertainment

Throughout the twentieth century, Mullingar had a rich cultural life with thriving theatre companies, musical societies and bands.

In 1896, the St Mary's Temperance Society Drama Class was formed. For decades the class was the main amateur theatre group in town, offering 'the youth and apprentices' of Mullingar the opportunity to develop their acting talents and gain self-confidence. Their very first production was *The White Horse of the Peppers* by Samuel Lover in 1896. Other productions included *The Colleen Bawn*, *Robert Emmett*, *The Irishman*, and in 1916, an ambitious twenty-six-scene version of *Oliver Twist*.

No women were allowed to appear on stage so the female roles were played by youths, as in Shakespeare's day! The dramatic class met, firstly in a building on the corner of Pearse and Mount Street later known as the Arcade, and then in premises in Church Lane formerly occupied by the Workingmen's Club and known as the Trade and Labour Hall.

The main venue for theatre productions in the first decade of the twentieth century was the lecture hall in Bishopsgate Street. From 1913, the County Hall in the new County Buildings became Mullingar's premier theatre. The first production put on there by the Temperance Society was *The Triumph of an Honest Man*. A major figure in the drama movement at this time was Frank Russell, who was both an actor and producer with the Temperance Society for decades.

The Parochial Hall in Church Avenue was another major cultural venue from its opening in 1888. A regular visitor to this hall was Dr Heuston Collier, organiser of the Dublin popular concerts in the ancient concert rooms and an expert on classical music. He was a friend and collaborator with Percy French and French was also a frequent visitor to Mullingar. One of his concerts in the Parochial Hall, on 25 September 1912, was a landmark occasion in the town's cultural history for it was on that occasion that 'Come Back Paddy Reilly' received its first performance – the *Westmeath Examiner* review of the concert described the ballad as, 'A song full of the true pathos and longing of the Irish exile for his home'.

In the aftermath of the First World War, the Mullingar Choral Society was formed. The society was the first to stage the works of Gilbert and Sullivan in Mullingar, beginning with *The Mikado* in January 1921. There was a repeat performance of this production in April 1922, which was made particularly memorable because, on opening night, 'The show was handicapped by being deprived of the County Hall at the last moment through it being taken over by Republican forces; and the cast and crew had to relocate to St Mary's Hall [formerly the lecture hall] in Bishopsgate Street.'

The Mikado was the first of many musical shows to be staged in the County Hall. There were further productions of Gilbert and Sullivan works during the interwar years, including *The Pirates of Penzance* in 1924, as well as *The Geisha* in 1937. Among those involved with the Choral Society were such notable Mullingar citizens as Dr Tony Stanley, Harry Gilbert and Fr Crinion. In the post-war era, the society would move into large-scale productions: *The Desert Song* in 1948; *Rose Marie* in 1950; *Bless the Bride* in 1953; *The Student Prince* in 1954; *The Desert Song* in 1956, and *South Pacific* in 1958. The President of Ireland and the American Ambassador were among those who attended Choral Society performances in the 1950s. Since the late 1960s, the society has concentrated on the production of choral works by Mozart, Bach, Fauré, etc. Most of these productions have taken place in the cathedral.

The Temperance Society closed down in 1935, but by then other drama companies had

Above: St Mary's Temperance Society Drama Club *c.*1906.

Below: Charity concert for Titanic victims in the Parochial hall, 1912.

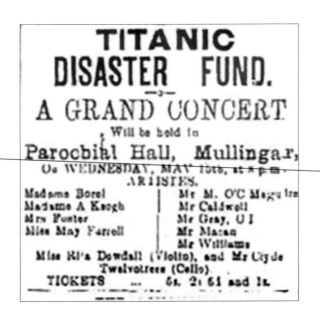

emerged. The Mullingar Gaelic League branch staged plays by Abbey Theatre writers and other Irish authors. During the 1916-23 Troubles, Gaelic League productions were often used to raise funds for the freedom struggle. The thirties saw the formation of the Mullingar Repertory players, whose members included Ambrose Walsh and Jack Seery.

At the start of the 1940s, the Little Theatre Group was formed. One of the founders was Dr Tony Stanley and one of the company's first productions was a play written by him called *Troubled Bachelors*. This comedy became very popular around Ireland with amateur companies and was highly praised. Another local writer involved with the company was Leo Daly, whose play *Death's Echo* was also staged by Little Theatre. The company won several awards and sponsored drama festivals. Members of the company included Packy Holmes, Peter Fagan, Des Braiden, Maggie Caffrey, the journalist Des Rushe and the novelist Josephine Harte.

Mullingar Players was another company, whose productions included *Judge Not*, written by its founder, Jack Seery. The Players won the Universal Cup in the Fr Matthew Feis with its production of *Gaslight* by Patrick Hamilton.

The St Loman's Players were formed in the 1960s and staged many pantomimes. Throughout the 1970s Revue shows were staged annually in the County Hall.

In 1978, the Mullingar Theatre Group was formed. Their opening production was *The Playboy of the Western World* and in 1982 they performed Brecht's *The Threepenny Opera*. This company included both veterans from the Little Theatre and Mullingar Players era, as well as a new generation of performers. The 1980s saw still more companies formed, including Lakeland Productions in 1984 and Wrymill Productions in 1989.

Many theatre companies and the stars of Irish and international stage visited Mullingar over the century. The Abbey Theatre company came several times and so did the Longford Players (founded by Edward and Christine Longford, the co-founders of the Gate Theatre). Cyril Cusack was another visitor. Indeed, it is probably true to say that nearly everyone who was and is everyone in the Irish acting profession has appeared in Mullingar – including Maureen Potter, Jimmy O'Dea, Noel Purcell and Ray McAnally. The actor and producer Anew McMaster was another visitor and those who attended his company's six-night tour of Mullingar in January 1952 would have seen the future Nobel Prize winner and playwright Harold Pinter, who was one of the cast. It should also be noted that some of those who first appeared on stage in Mullingar with the local drama companies and musical societies went on to make professional careers for themselves in theatre, including Pat Layde, who worked at the Abbey and appeared in several films, and Tina Kellegher, who has worked with the Abbey and Druid and appeared on film and TV.

One truly major literary figure with Mullingar connections was James Joyce. Joyce stayed in Mullingar for a number of weeks in 1900 and 1901, helping his father with the task of drawing up a new Electoral Register for the town. Joyce never forgot Mullingar. In his first novel, *Stephen Hero*, which he later rewrote as *A Portrait of the Artist as a Young Man*, there was a chapter set in Mullingar. The town is also mentioned in *Ulysses*, where Leopold Bloom's daughter, Milly Bloom, is working as a photographer's assistant in Mullingar and enjoying herself going to concerts in the Greville Arms and picnics at Lough Owel.

While in Mullingar Joyce wrote his first creative work, a play called *A Brilliant Career*, which he dedicated to himself! He later discarded the play, feeling it to be too derivative. It

Mullingar Choral Society production of *The Mikado* in the 1920s.

Members of the Choral Society in a production of *Salad Days* in 1963.

Mullingar Choral Society production of *The Student Prince* in the 1950s.
From left to right: T. Lyons, Nancy Savage, Tony Stanley, Sheela McCormack, Fr Crinion, Dotie Brophil, Pat Clohessy.

Celebrating the broadcast on RTÉ of a play about James Joyce in Mullingar. The authors, Bernard Share and Leo Daly, are second and third from the left.

Mullingar Choral Society

presents

THE MULLINGAR CHOIR

in their first

CHORAL CONCERT

County Hall, Mullingar

March 2nd, 1969

REQUIEM

(Gabriel Fauré)

THE GONDOLIERS

(Gilbert and Sullivan)

The Society thanks the Arts Council for its generous assistance

Above: Dr Tony Stanley and the cast of *Troubled Bachelors* in the 1940s.

Left: Choral Society programme, 1969.

Below: Mullingar Little Theatre production of the musical *The Bachelors* in 1965.

Above: A production of *Witness for the Prosecution* by the Mullingar Players in the 1950s.

Left: Kitty Corcoran was one of the stars of the Mullingar theatre and musical scene in the 1940s and 1950s.

ST. LOMAN'S PLAYERS

PRESENT THEIR SECOND ANNUAL
PANTOMIME

Aladdin

and his Wonderful Lamp

●

COUNTY HALL, MULLINGAR

FRIDAY, 21st FEBRUARY

TO SUNDAY, 1st MARCH,

AND

FRIDAY, 6th & SUNDAY, 8th MARCH, 1964
NIGHTLY AT 8.30 P.M.

●

SOUVENIR PROGRAMME .... 3d.

WESTMEATH EXAMINER LTD., MULLINGAR

Right: Programme for a St Loman's
Players Production.

Below: Members of the St Loman's
Players in the 1970s.

Members of a Lakeland production rehearse *Godspell* in 1992.

SUNDAY, 17th OCTOBER, 1948

ALL-STAR VARIETY CONCERT

With — ARTANE SCHOOL BOYS' BAND, DUBLIN
(Conducted by John W. Hickey); JOHN THOMPSON
(Radio Eireann Tenor); MIKE NOLAN (Comedian—Minto's
Cagtime Band); EILEEN O'CONNELL (Soprano); LEO
ROWSOME (Famous Uileann Piper); GILLIE FOX
(Tenor—Athlone Musical Society); KATHLEEN HYNES
(Juvenile Star); MICK FOX (Merry Minstrel—Banjo—
Capitol Theatre). Show Compered by BART BASTABLE
(Chief Announcer, Hospital Trust Sponsored Programme)

* * *

ADMISSION — — — 3/6 (Reserved) AND 2/-
Booking opens on 3rd October. 2/- Tickets on sale.

Advertisment for a variety concert, 1948.

Above: Mullingar pays tribute to RTÉ's first TV newsreader.

Below: In the 1950s the Abbey Theatre Company visited Mullingar.

After two and a half years in Australia,

Personal Appearance of

Anew McMaster

And His International Company

In The County Hall, Mullingar

(For Six Nights Only)

Monday, 28th Jan., to Saturday, 2nd Feb.

Monday	**Lady Windermere's Fan** (by Oscar Wilde)
Tuesday	**Othello**
Wednesday	**Love From a Stranger** (by Agatha Christie)
Thursday (Matinee 3 p.m.)	**The Merchant of Venice**
Thursday Night	**An Ideal Husband**
Friday	**Hamlet**
Saturday	**The Taming of the Shrew**

Nightly at 8.30.   Seats bookable at 3/6

ANEW McMASTER.

After two and a half years in Australia Mr. Anew McMaster and his International Company have returned to Ireland and played in the Co. Hall, Mullingar last week.

The Company had originally intended staying in Australia for six months but were forced to remain for two and a half years, by public demand.

Mr. McMaster appeared in his most famous role—that of Othello —a part he has played in all the great cities of the world. In Melbourne he was hailed as one of the greatest living Shakesperian actors ranking with Olivier, Gieland, Richardson.

All the productions were newly costumed, and the most modern stage lighting had been obtained. The Company included Miss Laurel Streeter, Sydney; Penelope Parry, Montreal; Harold Pinter, Ken Haig, John Mayes and Don Coulon (London); Joseph Nolan from Dublin, Pauline Flanagan Sligo; Jock Aronson from San Francisco Wm. Hay; Jerome Breheny, Patrick Gardiner.

The Company also incldes Miss Mary Rose McMaster, daughter of the famous Actor, who appeared as Desdemona to her father's Othello for the first time.

Above: Harold Pinter was one of the company on this visit to Mullingar in 1952.

Left: Harold Pinter is listed among the cast of Anew McMaster's Theatre Company in Mullingar, 1952.

Right: Actor Pat Layde on his wedding day, pictured with Vincent Dowling of the Abbey Theatre.

Locally born actress Tina Kellegher at the launch of the events programme at Mullingar Arts Centre. From left to right: Peter Fagan, Tina Kellegher, Brigid Kellegher, Christy Neary.

has been suggested by Leo Daly in his study *James Joyce and the Mullingar Connection*, that the play's theme, a young doctor struggling to deal with a plague in his town caused by sewage problems, was, in part, suggested by the major sewerage and drainage problems then afflicting Mullingar.

A statue of Joyce is now located in the Greville Arms Hotel (mentioned in his writings) and in the name of the 'Ulysses' Bar, as well as by a plaque in the Market House. Other famous writers to visit Mullingar included the novelist Evelyn Waugh and the poet John Betjeman.

In the second half of the century, the writer JP Dunleavy, author of *The Gingerman*, came to live in Mullingar. There is a connection between Joyce and Dunleavy, in that Dunleavy's home, Levington Park, an early-nineteenth-century mansion at Lough Owel, was possibly where Joyce stayed during his time in Mullingar. It was then the home of W.C. Levinge, the County Secretary.

Cinema became another important part of Mullingar's cultural life from the 1890s. Touring cinemas such as Tofts Electric Picture Palace showed films in a booth at the Fair Green, including a silent version of the Wagner opera *Siegfried*.

The Parochial Hall played host to the Irish Motion Picture Syndicate. The first show put on in the County Hall when it opened in 1913 was a film called *From the Manger to the Cross*, which caused controversy because the Virgin Mary was played by a divorced actress!

In January 1914, Mullingar's first cinema opened in Dominick Street. A second cinema, the Grand National Picture Palace was opened later the same year. The first 'talkies' were shown in

MULLINGAR JAMES JOYCE CENTENARY COMMITTEE
1982
PRESENTS

Haveth Music eVerywhere

An Encounter with Music and *Song in the Life and Works of*
JAMES JOYCE (1882-1941)

Performed as a Centenary Commemoration Presentation during

The VIII International James Joyce Symposium 1982

PREMIER PERFORMANCES IN:
GREVILLE ARMS HOTEL, MULLINGAR *at 8 p.m.*
Saturday, March 20th; Sunday, March 21st; Monday, March 22nd
Prices: Saturday Night (Students) £1; Sunday Night (including buffet) £5;
Monday Night (including Souvenir Programme) £2.50
Performances also at Galway University, Galway, and at other venues on dates to be arranged during Centenary Year, 1982.

Celebrating James Joyce's Centenary and his Mullingar connections in 1982.

the town in 1932 and a new cinema, the Hibernian, opened in Castle Street in 1947. Mullingar people showed the same enthusiasm for Hollywood stars as the rest of the world and 'the pictures' provided a welcome escape during times of economic hardship. In 1947, parts of the film *Captain Boycott* were filmed in Mullingar and in 1978, Sean Connery and Donald Sutherland were in town to film scenes for *The First Great Train Robbery*.

Bands and choirs also contributed to cultural life. The various British Army regiments in the barracks often supplied musical entertainment. For example, the string band of the Oxford Light Infantry played during the interval at a production of *The Colleen Bawn* in the lecture hall in 1899 and, in 1900, the string band of the Cameron Highlanders 'played some very nice selections' during a production of *The Wicklow Wedding* by the Temperance Society.

By 1906, the Mullingar Brass and Reed Band, all of whose members were teetotalers, were also providing music at productions by the Temperance Society. The musical director was George Rousse, a former military bandsman. He was also in charge of the asylum band.

What is now known as 'Mullingar Town Band' has, as Mullingar band historian Philip Tierney noted, 'Become an essential part of all important public occasions', providing musical entertainment, greeting visiting dignitaries and performing at sporting and cultural events.

From 1957 onwards under its Director, Hubert Magee, girls were admitted to the band. The band was there for the 1966 Golden Jubilee of the Rising celebrations, for the celebrations of the Westmeath Minor Footballers All-Ireland Championship in 1995, for the ceremonies welcoming the new millennium, and for many other events of historical significance. It also travelled widely and won a number of awards.

Classical music flourished in Mullingar throughout the twentieth century. The most important classical performance put on in the town was undoubtedly the Irish premiere of *The Dream of Gerontius* in the cathedral in 1958, which featured the Hallé Orchestra conducted by Sir John Barbirolli. In 1980, the Ulster Orchestra came to town. At the start of the twentieth century the Ester-Grime Opera Company came annually to Mullingar, putting on productions in the Parochial Hall. Towards the end of the century, Mullingar-born Ailish Tynan began

Josephine Hart signing books in Mullingar in 1991.

her distinguished career as a soprano, winning the RTÉ Millennium Singer of the Year award.

Irish culture has long had an enthusiastic following in Mullingar. In the early 1900s, as the Gaelic Revival took hold, organisations such as the Gaelic League and the Christian Brothers organised Irish music and dance events. Each summer from around 1906, a feis was held in the grounds of St Mary's CBS and many people from the town attended an Aéridhacht on the historic hill of Uishneach near Mullingar.

In 1951, Comhaltas Ceoltóirí Éireann was founded following a meeting in the Midland Hotel in Mount Street in 1951. Among the Mullingar founder members of Comhaltas were Kathleen Moynihan, Philip Mullally, Eamonn Moynihan and Brother Redmond.

The first Feis Laír na hÉireann was held in the town in April 1951. In 1963, Mullingar played host to the All-Ireland Fleadh. Over 100,000 people came to

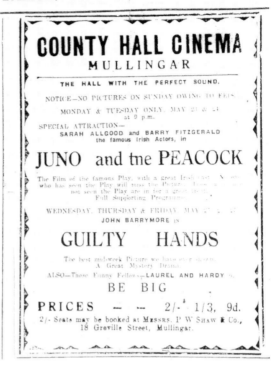

In the 1930s one of Mullingar's cinemas was in the County Hall.

Mullingar for the event, probably the largest crowd ever assembled in the town in its history. Despite the trouble caused by a small number of revellers, most people enjoyed a fine display of the best of traditional music and dance. Comhaltas is still active all year round in Mullingar. Traditional music has also flourished thanks to the work of Cairde na Cruite (Friends of the Harp), the Harp school founded in Mullingar in 1985. For many years, an annual concert celebrating the harp took place in the Officers' Mess at Columb Barracks.

In the field of popular music, the early sixties marked the start of a golden age for bands from Mullingar as the showband era took hold. Bands played weekly in venues such as the County Hall, the Lake County Hotel and The Lakeland (later Horizon) Ballroom.

Visiting stars included Johnny Cash and Lulu. But by the end of the decade, Mullingar had produced its own star, with Joe Dolan taking the national and international pop world by storm. Dolan, who began his forty-year career as one of Ireland's top entertainers with the band Joe Dolan and the Drifters, was probably the most famous Mullingar person of the twentieth century and was the only Irish artist to have chart hits in all five decades from the 1960s through to the 2000s. At the start of the new millennium, he was still entertaining his huge fan club with albums such as 21st Century Joe. His funeral in December 2007 saw the biggest crowds in Mullingar since the 1963 Fleadh.

Tommy and Jimmy Swarbrigg were not natives of Westmeath, but they settled in Mullingar

An army band in Dominick Street before 1910.

and made a major contribution to the music scene. Playing first with The Drifters, they then founded the Times Showband, before playing as The Swarbriggs. In 1977, they put Mullingar on the international musical map when they were chosen to represent Ireland in the Eurovision Song Contest

Foster and Allen were another Mullingar act to achieve prominence in the 1970s and 1980s. Larry Caffrey's bar in Mount Street became an important venue for many local musicians in the seventies and early eighties.

Finally, art also played a role in the cultural history of Mullingar. In the mid-twentieth century there was John Kelly RHA, who did the fine painting of Saint Colman in the cathedral museum. In 1964, the Mullingar Art Guild was founded and has staged an annual exhibition ever since. Other art groups followed, and by the late 1990s, the County Hall, renamed the Arts Centre, had a gallery.

The (seemingly faceless) Asylum band and choir, in a photograph taken around 1900.

The town band leading old IRA Veterans to Ballyglass for Easter Sunday Commemoration, March 1951.

RTÉ personality Micheál Ó'Muircheartaigh leading the town band during the filming of an RTÉ documentary.

The town band and director Hubert Magee in the Town Park, early 1980s.

Above: Singer Ailish Tynan giving a recital in London.

Right: The 1909 Mullingar Féis was backed by Mullingar's leading citizens at the time, when support for Irish cultural nationalism was growing.

ꝼeir Láin na h-éireann.

Sunday & Monday, 11th and 12th July, 1909.

Patron—The Most Rev. LAURENCE GAUGHRAN, D.D., Lord Bishop of Meath.

Rev. P. DALY, Adm., President

J. P. DOWDALL, M.C.C. } Treasurers.
PATRICK KEELAN, J.P.

SECRETARIES

General Secretary—Tomár Dubnal (T. J. Dowdall, Ll.D.)
Literary Section—Seáṡan Ó Catáin (J. J. Keane.)
Industrial Section—Máiṡṫéan Dubnal (Miss Dowdall.)
Dancing Section—Seóraṫ Ó Connaċṫáin (Jos. Connaughton.)

COMMITTEE :

Rev. J. L. Magee, C.C. ; Rev. B. O'Farrell, C.C. ; Rev H. Carpenter, C.C. ; Rev. J. Kelly, C.C. ; Rev. M. Dillon, C.C. ; Very Rev D. Flynn, President St. Finian's College, Mullingar ; Rev P. Duffy, Vice-President, do. ; Rev J. Flynn, Professor, do. ; Rev J. Lynam do., do. ; Rev M. M'Manus, do. do. ; Rev M. Hughes, do., do. ; Rev. W. Falkiner, Miss Mooney, Mrs. J J King, Miss Macken Mrs. Delamere, Mrs. Thomas F. Nooney, Mrs. J. Doyle, Mrs. O'Connell, Mrs. Patrick J. Nooney, Mrs Robertson, Mrs. John J. Macken, Mrs. Patrick J. Weymes, Mrs. J P. M'Cormack, Misses Maguire, Misses Keelan, Miss B. Doherty, Miss Dowdall, Miss Farrell, Miss Ward, Miss Kilcullen, John P. Hayden, M.P. ; A. J. Kearney, M.D. ; O. P. Kerrigan, M.D. ; N. J. Downes, J. J. Macken, R. J. Downes, Chairman Co. Council ; J. Tuite, J.P. ; T. J. Shaw, J.P. ; Owen Wickham, J.P. ; Patrick Maguire, T. L. Hutchinson, N. T. McNaboe, Co. Co. ; Michael Ward, P. Cleary, J. Brett, J. T. Roche, J. P. M'Cormack, P. Connellan, Leo M'Cormack, P J Weymes, J.P, C.T.C ; T Coleman, J Connaughton M Maguire, P. Shanahan, E. Murphy, William Barry, D.C ; J. P. Dowdall, Co. Co; M. Keelan, H Burke, John Murray, Kenny ; J. Tynan, T. J. Macken, S. O'Halloran, J. J. King, J. G Gibbon, M.D ; F. Delamere, T. F. Nooney, J.P. ; J. J. Keane, T. J. Dowdall, Ll.D ; J. Doyle, M. J. Kelly.

*Above:*Visitors to the Fleadh Ceoil of 1963 camping in the People's Park.

Below: Comhaltas Ceoltóirí Éireann dancers in the Market Square, 1992.

Above: Rachel McGuinness School of Dancers, 1994.

Below: Local traditional musicians in the Lake County celebrating the opening of T Na G in 1996.

LAKELAND BALLROOM, MULLINGAR

WHERE ONLY THE BEST BANDS PLAY

SUNDAY NEXT, 6th OCTOBER

THE FABULOUS

WOODCHOPPERS SHOWBAND

FROM DERRY

DANCING 9—1   ADMISSION   6/-

Coming Attraction — 13th October — THE ROYAL
October 15th — JOHNNY CASH

LAKELAND, MULLINGAR

TUESDAY, 15th OCTOBER

WORLD'S No. 1 COUNTRY & WESTERN SINGER

JOHNNY CASH

Seller of over eleven million records including his
fantastic Irish hit "FORTY SHADES OF GREEN"

JUNE CARTER

AMERICA'S GLAMOROUS COUNTRY & WESTERN QUEEN
By arrangement with the Irish Federation of Musicians

Roseland Ballroom, Moate

TO-NIGHT (FRIDAY)

THE DRIFTERS SHOWBAND

SUNDAY NEXT, 6th OCTOBER

THE SENSATIONAL

DIXIELANDERS Showband, Cork

STARS OF RADIO, T.V. AND DECCA RECORDS

DANCING 9 P.M.   ADMISSION   6/-

THE MELODY ACES

AT

Longford Arms Ballroom

THURSDAY NEXT, 10th OCTOBER

Johnny Cash in Mullingar, 1963.

Mick Foster singing in Larry Caffrey's Pub in the 1970s.

ST. MARY'S HALL COMMITTEE

H O P

ST. MARY'S HALL, MULLINGAR

ON FRIDAY, 21st MAY, 1965

FIREHOUSE FIVE

ancing: 8 — 12   ::   ADMISSION 3
RIGHT OF ADMISSION RESERVED.

A Mullingar 'Hop' in 1965.

The Drifters Show Band, 1960s.

Dinny Hughes and his orchestra in 1963.

One of Joe Dolan's biggest hits.

five

Sport

Sport has played a major part in Mullingar life for centuries and during the last one hundred years the variety of sports played in the town has increased and more women and girls have had the opportunity to get involved.

Gaelic sports such as hurling and football began to be played in an organised manner in Westmeath from the late 1880s, following the founding of the GAA in 1884. The first GAA meeting in Mullingar took place on 17 October 1889 and this led to the setting up of a Mullingar Branch of the GAA and of a club generally known as the Mullingar Commercials, who played their first gaelic football match in Ballyglass area of the town on 20 October that year. Within a year, three more clubs were formed and matches were played, mainly in winter, at various venues around the town. But many of the players also played cricket and soccer and it was not until the early 1900s that clubs in town began to play gaelic football exclusively and to exclude those who played so-called 'English' games.

By the summer of 1903 there were six Mullingar football teams: Young Ireland, Mullingar Shamrocks, Cullion Celtics, Railway Stars, Newbrook Wanderers and Independent Wanderers. A Westmeath County GAA Committee was founded in February 1905 at a meeting in Mullingar attended by thirteen clubs, with Patrick Murphy of the Young Ireland Club as President, Anthony Conniffe of Shamrocks as Secretary and Philip Mullaly of Cullion as Treasurer.

The first hurling club in Mullingar was set up by St Mary's Temperance Club in February 1902 and the first hurling match in the town took place on St Patrick's Day 1903, when Shamrocks Club beat a visiting team from Longford. The match was played at the Newbrook racecourse and Shamrocks became Westmeath's first county hurling champions in 1904.

The growth in gaelic football and hurling coincided with the rise of Nationalism, and the GAA in Mullingar, as elsewhere, became linked with other Nationalist organisations such as the Gaelic League, the Ancient Order of Hibernians and the IRB and Irish Volunteers. Many of those who played and supported gaelic games would be involved in the War of Independence and were watched by the RIC. During the early years of the century too, gaelic games began to be played in schools, with St Finian's, for example, putting gaelic football on its sports curriculum right from its foundation in Mullingar in 1908. This helped Westmeath to win Leinster Junior Football Championships in 1905 and 1915 and the Junior Hurling Championship in 1912. A past pupil of St Mary's, Paddy Bracken, would play a key role in helping Westmeath to win the All-Ireland Minor Championship in 1929.

One of the most significant days in the history of the GAA in Mullingar was 16 July 1933, when Cusack Park grounds opened. Teams from all over the county paraded through the town and a plane flew over the grounds before the inaugural match between Cavan and Meath. Another important day was 14 August 1938, when Michael O'Hehir, the man destined to be 'the voice of gaelic sport' for almost fifty years, made his very first broadcast from Cusack Park, when he covered the All-Ireland Senior Semifinal.

By the second half of the century, Mullingar had a number of football and hurling teams including St Loman's (formerly known as Mental Hospital) Shamrocks, Cullions and St Oliver Plunkett's. Both St Loman's and Shamrocks became major teams at county level, winning several championships and providing players for the county teams. In 1963, Westmeath won the Leinster minor football and junior hurling titles and the CBS and St Finian's teams also began to make an impact. As the town and county began to become more

Springfield Stars (Mental Hospital, Mullingar) Senior Football team of 1925/26. Back row, left to right, Tom Clinton, Jack Bardon, John Creamer, Mick Mulvihill, Willie Brown, Frank Moran and Hugh Tormey. Front row, from left, Joe Morrison, Jim Lyster, Tom Commons, Terry Caffrey, Phil Gaynor, Pat Devine and Paddy Creamer.

The Mental Hospital (Springfield) Gaelic football team 1925-1926.

prosperous in the sixties and seventies, Cusack Park was improved with the building of the stand in 1963 and dressing rooms. Clubhouses were built by Shamrocks, Oliver Plunkett's, St Loman's and Cullion, and players no longer needed to tog out in pubs before heading to Cusack Park. By the early 1980s it was estimated that Westmeath GAA properties were worth more than £1 million (punts).

In the last decades of the twentieth century, GAA sports continued to grow throughout Mullingar with almost all local schools playing football, hurling or camogie, and teams such as Shamrocks and St Loman's continuing to win county championships at senior and junior level.

The introduction of the Scór competition in the 1970s added to the upsurge in interest in the GAA in Mullingar and the Community Games, started in 1972, also encouraged interest in sport. For female players and fans, the last decades of the twentieth century saw improved opportunities. Camogie had been played since the early part of the century in Mullingar but really took off from the 1970s onwards, with teams such as Cullion. In 1974, Ladies Gaelic Football was inaugurated in Ireland and what is now the country's fastest growing sport was played in Mullingar by schools and clubs from the 1980s. In 1995, for example, St Loman's Ladies Footballers were senior 'B' champions and in 1998 Shamrocks won the county championships.

In 1995, Westmeath won the All-Ireland Minor Football Championship and most of Mullingar thronged the streets to welcome the victorious team home to a reception in the town park. In 1999, it was the turn of the U21 team to win All-Ireland Championship glory and these victories made the maroon and white Westmeath colours familiar throughout the town to a new generation and helped pave the way for further glory in the new century, when Westmeath became Leinster Senior Football Champions and Christy Ring Cup Hurling Winners.

In Mullingar, rugby was first played at the Military Barracks in the nineteenth and early

Cullion—Minor Hurling Champions. Back row, from left, Gerry Gillen, Denis Burke, James Keegan, Joe Martin, Sean Scanlon, Camillus Walsh, Gerry Carr, Pat Carolan, Denis Corroon. Front row, from left, Michael Hynes, George Savage, Ultan Tuite, John J. Lynch, Joe Lynam, Larry Maguire, Seamus Devine, John Corroon, and Ger Heery.

Cullion Minor Hurlers in 1975.

Shamrocks Westmeath Senior Football Champions team, 1964.
Back row, from left to right: Frankie Connaughton, Frichin McCormack, Ollie Mulvey, Brendan McNamara, Davy Nolan, Jim Finn, Vincent Lennon, Paddy Cole, Tommy Lennon, Jim O'Dowd.
Front row: Mousie Mullen, Tommy Carrigh, Colm Connaughton, Sean Magee, Terry O'Dowd, Kevin Higgins, Dan O'Dowd, Pat McCormack, Willo Reynolds.

The St. Lomans Under-12 team for 1988: *Front row, left to right, Simon Corroon, David McKinley, Kenny Maleady, Cathal Lyons, James Davit, Frank Shaw, Gary Devine, Billy Murtagh. Back row, left to right, Harry Devine (Trainer), Aidan Croagh, Ciaran Foxe, Brendan Brady, Henry Abbott, Alan Quinn, Johnny Forbes, Ciaran Heffernan, Kevin Craig (Trainer).*

St Loman's U12 Gaelic Football team in 1988.

twentieth centuries, and was also apparently briefly played at St Finian's College after its foundation. But it was not until 1925 that Mullingar Rugby Club was founded following a meeting at the Central Hotel in Oliver Plunkett Street. Games were played at the Mullingar showgrounds until the opening of the Rugby Club Pavilion and Grounds at Cullion on the northern edge of the town in 1977.

Throughout the thirties, rugby remained a minority sport in the town and a shortage of players almost put paid to the club at one point. But during the Second World War, the game became popular with the army and LDF personnel at the barracks and in April 1944 an army team beat a civilian team in a match played at the camp field beside the barracks. This gave new life to Mullingar Rugby Club, which was reactivated following a meeting in the County Hall in September of 1944. The most significant player of the era in Mullingar was army despatch rider Roche T. who played for eight senior clubs in his time and was once described by one of his teammates as 'being to Mullingar RFC what Willie John McBride means to Ballymena'.

In 1954, Mullingar won the Leinster Cup, beating Naas 3-0 in Tullamore. The Mullingar men won again in 1956 and also won the inaugural midland league in 1958. By the last years of the century, rugby had become a very popular sport in Mullingar and was being played in schools as well as at adult level. In the 1990s the Mullingar Club reached two town's cup finals.

The earliest reference to soccer being played in Mullingar goes back to 1878, when a match took place in the camp field. At the beginning of the twentieth century, members of a gaelic football team called Newbrook Wanderers also played soccer as St Patrick's Club, with matches taking place at the Newbrook racecourse grounds. St Patrick's, which started

Oliver Plunkett Club Hurlers on parade in 1988.

playing soccer in 1899, can therefore probably be considered to be Mullingar's first soccer team. Many of the players had watched soccer being played at the army barracks. But they seem not to have had much talent, with one reporter describing them as having 'plenty of vigour but lacked every other quality'. The club broke up in 1905 and another team, Glenmore, was then formed.

But the growth of soccer in Mullingar was severely hampered by the rise of a narrow-minded Nationalism which deemed the playing of 'English' games such as soccer to be unpatriotic. As early as 1905, following one poorly attended soccer match in the town, the *Midland Reporter* claimed that gaelic sport 'had certainly killed the imported game in the Co. Westmeath'. The GAA 'ban' on playing and watching 'foreign' games also damaged soccer because the overwhelming majority of Mullingar soccer players and supporters came from Roman Catholic backgrounds – the same background as the GAA and the Nationalists.

Nevertheless, soccer continued to be played in Mullingar down through the twentieth century and after the lifting of the 'ban' in 1971, the numbers of players and supporters increased. Mullingar never enjoyed the same level of success as the teams in Athlone did but, in 1973, Mullingar Town Soccer Club achieved glory when they defeated St Francis (Dublin) at Athlone to win the Glen Abbey Cup. The win, by three goals to two, was all the more impressive given that the Mullingar men ended the match with only ten men. The team, captained by Frankie Murray, were given a triumphant homecoming to Mullingar, greeted by the town band and Mrs Power's Accordion Band and by the Town Commissioners, County Councillors and TDs. Mullingar Town was the first club from outside Dublin to win the Glen Abbey Cup.

Cullion Camogie Minor team, 1990s.
Back row, from left to right: Andrea Martin, Lorraine Gilhooley, Jackie White, Teres Allen, Una Fagan, Valerie Reynolds, Pauline Hogan, Ashling Reynolds, Roisin McCool, Sharon Monaghan.
Front: Emma Martin, Roseanna Leavy, Gemma Mahon, Sinead Marshall, Caroline Sharry, Aoife Davitt, Hiliary Corcoran, Siofra Murtagh.

This picture was taken at the presentation of medals to O Growney Tce., Mullingar, under 10 football team after they had won the Mullingar Street League. Back row, from left, Mr. Sean Nolan, Chairman, Mullingar G.A.A.; Mr. Tommy Gilhooley, Mr. Paul McGrath and Mr. Tommy Lennon. Front row, from left, Patrick Fitzgerald, Paul Early, Joe Gilhooley, O'Growney Tce. captain and Sean Murphy.

O'Growney Terrace players, winners of the under ten Mullingar Street League Football Championship.

Oliver Plunketts — Westmeath Intermediate Hurling Championship Runners-Up in 1988. *Front row, left to right, Noel Farley, Sean Hynes, Pat Gorman, Kevin Kiernan, David Cornally, J. J. Lynch, John McDonnell (Capt.), Brian Gaye, Terry Lacey, Paul Ahearne, Paddy Casey, Eddie Casey, Noel Gavin. Back row, left to right, Paddy Boyce, Gerry Rafter, Brian Smith, Brendan Lyons, Tom Bawle, Eoghan Flanagan, Michael Coyle, Joe Bustin, John Hassett, Ray McDonnell, Paul Moran, Davy Gavin, Alan Reidy, Declan Mooney, Johnny Keating, Pat Hassett, Tony Donoghue. Mascots, David Lynch, John Paul McDonnell.*

Oliver Plunkett's Hurling Club, Westmeath Intermediate Hurlers Runners-up, 1988.

The group 'Clann Lir', winners of the Scór Championship in 1976.
From left to right: Dick Hogan, Colman Moynihan, Caroline Crinnigan, Noel Battle.

Shamrocks Ladies Footballers U16 team celebrate winning the County Championship in 1998.
From left to right: Aideen Martin, Louise Begley, Marie Monaghan, Sarah Graham, Linda Gilmartin, Lisa
Burke, Elaine Golfer, Lorraine Casserly, Geraldine Giles.

Westmeath All-Ireland Minor Football Champions return to Mullingar, 1995.

One famous Mullingar Town player in the 1940s and 1950s was Maxie McCullough. As well as soccer, McCullough was also a boxer and won the Lightweight Championship in boxing at the European Championships in Norway in 1949, as well as being part of the Irish Team at the 1948 Olympics in London.

Mullingar Town have their grounds at Dalton Park. A second soccer team was founded in 1983 in Mullingar with the birth of Mullingar Athletic Club, which played its first match in Ballinea. Early games and training took place in St Finian's College grounds and in the Grange area, until a new ground was made at Gainstown, just south of Mullingar, in 1987. A string of successes followed at Leinster Football League level and at Premier Division, from 1987 onwards.

Cricket was probably the most popular sport in Westmeath in the nineteenth century, with Mullingar the base of the County Club. Matches, often played against visiting army regiments, were played in places such as Ballinderry and the asylum grounds. At the start of the twentieth century, there were also teams representing occupations or other sectional interests in the town. The staff at the asylum fielded a team, as did the Temperance Society, the Catholic Commercial Club and the National Workingmen's Club. Some clubs played cricket in summer and gaelic football in winter.

In the early 1900s Nationalists in Mullingar increasingly turned against cricket. The game, popular with the Fenians in the nineteenth century, was now seen as foreign and players were ridiculed and abused as 'West Britons' and anti-national. By the First World War, the cricket clubs of the town were reinventing themselves as Gaelic football or hurling clubs. But cricket did survive, and by the end of the century, the arrival of immigrants from such cricketing nations as India, Pakistan and South Africa meant that the game was getting a new lease of life.

Athletics has a long history in Mullingar and a distinguished one. Army regiments and St Mary's CBS held athletic contests and the RIC and members of the Catholic Commercial Club and National Workingmen's Club were also involved in competitions. In July 1898, the World Long Jump Champion, Westmeath-born Walter Newburn jumped 24ft 6¾in at an IAAA meeting at Newbrook racecourse. This was a world record although never recorded as such. Newburn's jumping board, draped in a Union Jack, was displayed in the window of Gordon's Drapery Store.

Another world-class athlete of the time was Peter O'Connor, who worked in Mullingar as a solicitor's clerk. He won a total of eight amateur athletic titles between 1901 and 1906 and won Gold and Silver medals at the 1906 Olympic games. In August 1901, he set a world record in the long jump which would survive until 1921 and would not be broken as an Irish record until 1990. He used to train at a venue near Piper's Boreen in the Millmount area of Mullingar, although he had left the town by the time of his world record and Olympic triumphs. Mullingar Athletic and Cycling Club emerged in the early 1900s involving many members of the Temperance Society. Over the years many top-class Irish athletes came to compete in Mullingar and the town produced many athletes. The Athletic and Cycling Club were followed by Mullingar Harriers, whose members have also included successful athletes such as Martin Fagan. In 1983, Harriers member Bobby Begley managed the Irish team at the World Championships in Helsinki at which Eamonn Coughlan won the 5,000m title.

Horse racing has been going on in Mullingar for at least two centuries and in 1852 the

Newbrook racecourse opened. This course fell into disuse in the 1880s but was revived in 1890 by a number of local businessmen and landowners. By June 1902 race goers were able to avail of special trains, which delivered them to a siding at the course, and up to 13,000 attended the June meeting in 1903. An annual horse show was held from 1894. In 1913, Mullingar Racecourse Company shareholders received a 10 per cent dividend.

The racecourse survived the First World War and an entertainments tax brought in by the new Free State Government in the 1920s. Mullingar men Robert Downes and T.J. Dowdell were key figures in the world of Irish racing in the interwar era. In 1939, when Newbrook received a £10,000 grant from the government to boost prize money, a national newspaper described Mullingar racecourse as 'more popular than ever'.

During the Second World War, Newbrook was closed but it reopened in 1946 with five meetings. The two-day June meet with its Mullingar Gold Cup was seen as a 'stepping stone to the Galway Plate'.

By the sixties, however, the racecourse was running at a loss and in 1967, the final race was run with 'Moigh Star' trained by local man Eamonn Finn as the final winner. Six years earlier, the great horse Arkle, ridden by Mark Hely Hutchinson, came in third at a meeting at Newbrook on 9 December 1961.

Local horses have also won many great races, most notably 'Quare Times', winner of the English Grand National in 1955. Mullingar horses also won the 1900 and 1902 Irish Grand Nationals.

Polo was played in the Mullingar area in the era prior to the First World War. Indeed, in 1896 Westmeath were All-Ireland Polo Champions and in 1908, a team drawn largely from the Mullingar area beat Meath in the All-Ireland semi-finals. The polo grounds were at Ledeston near Lough Ennell. Most of the players were from the local landowning class, but the Asylum Medical Officer, Dr Finnegan and the County Surveyor, A.E. Joyce also played, as did some army officers.

Mullingar Golf Club was founded in 1894, following a meeting at the Greville Arms Hotel. The first course, opened in 1895, was at Newbrook racecourse but in 1900 moved to Mount Prospect on the Dublin Road. In 1909, the club moved to a course along the Lynn Road and then in 1919, following long disputes with the landowner Thomas Roche over issues such as the application of fertiliser to the fairways, the grazing of horses on the course and whose responsibility it was to till land seized by the government for compulsory tillage, the Golf Club moved to lands at Lough Owel.

The Lough Owel course was opened in July 1919. The first ball was driven by the Lady Captain, Gwen Nooney. It was a beautiful course but the fact that the rail line to Sligo ran through the middle did cause problems. On one occasion a ball landed in a passing goods wagon and was carried six miles – possibly the longest drive in golfing history.

In 1935, the club moved yet again, to lands belonging to Colonel Charles Howard-Bury of Belvedere. This has been its home ever since. Famous members over the years include Eddie Jordan, who worked as a bank official in Mullingar in the sixties and seventies (he was also Secretary of Mullingar Go-Karting Club), Walker Cup Champion David Sheehan and Joe Dolan. Mullingar Golf Club also won numerous prizes in competitions over the decades and hosted major players such as Fred Daly, British Open Winner, who ran the Irish Professional Championship at Mullingar in 1952. In recent years, Padraig Harrington, Darren Clarke and

MULLINGAR RUGBY FOOTBALL CLUB, INAUGURAL SEASON, 1925/6. Back row, left to right, T. P. Downes, M. Greally, T. Shaw, J. Hope, Garda J. Duffy, F. Brabazon, J. R. Downes. Sitting, S. K. Brabazon, ..., J. O'Hara, Sergt. J. Brophy (Capt.), J. Hennessy .... In front, A. Lougheed, P. McCarroll.

First Mullingar Rugby Football Club team in 1925-26.

Rugby players at the army barracks in the 1950s.

Rugby team at Newbrook, 1950.

Paul McGinley have also played in Mullingar at the Scratch Club.

Tennis was played in Mullingar from the late nineteenth century, and a tennis club existed at Millmount Road, on the site of what is now the Community College, from around the 1890s. Mullingar Town Tennis Club was established in 1936, on the present club site. By the seventies, tennis was one of Mullingar's most popular sports and was being played in many of the town's schools. Loreto College's minor team won the Leinster Cup in 1981 and St Mary's CBS won the Junior Colleges' Boys Cup, among many other achievements. From the 1970s until the early 2000s tennis balls were actually manufactured in Mullingar, at the Penn Factory.

Both golf and tennis offered women in Mullingar opportunities to take part in sport from the 1890s onwards. Cycling and hunting also gave women a chance to compete. Fox hunting, still practiced in Mullingar, is possibly the longest established sport in the area, going back to the seventeenth century. The Hunt Ball was one of the highlights of the social year.

Numerous other sports have been played in Mullingar over the last century – too many to cover in detail; squash, pitch and putt, hockey, handball, yachting, swimming, snooker, basketball, greyhound racing and karate are just some of these sports. Boxing in Mullingar attracted players from the military and from all sections of Mullingar society. In 1943, Chris Cole defeated former Champion Jack Doyle ('The Gorgeous Gael') in two minutes at Dalymount Park. Maxie McCullagh, already mentioned, was European Lightweight Champion in 1949. By the end of the century, members of Mullingar's Traveller Community were making a major contribution to boxing in the town and winning national and international titles.

Finally, swimming is worthy of particular mention. Generations of Mullingar children learned to swim in the Royal Canal and the lakes that surround Mullingar. But it was in 1948 that a number of local people, without any national or local government funding, managed to set up a swimming/diving club at Lough Owel, which opened with a Swimming Gala in August 1948.

For many years, the Lough Owel Swimming Club was the town's main venue for swimmers and divers and is still in existence today. In 1972, a new swimming pool opened in the town park. Mullingar swimmers have achieved international and national success.

Junior soccer players in 1921.

Mullingar Town Soccer Club win the Glen Abbey Cup in 1973.

Mullingar Town AFC in 1973.

MAXIE McCULLAGH WELCOMED HOME

MAXIE McCULLAGH RECEIVED A ROUSING WEL-
COME IN MULLINGAR ON SATURDAY NIGHT ON
HIS FIRST VISIT TO HIS NATIVE TOWN AFTER WIN-
NING THE AMATEUR LIGHT-WEIGHT CHAMPIONSHIP
OF EUROPE AT OSLO.

So vast was the crowd which thronged the vicinity of the Green Bridge that Gardaí had to control the traffic. Mullingar Brass and Reed Band and Mullingar Boys' Pipe Band marched to the station, followed by large singing and cheering crowds to meet and greet the champion. The Tricolour was displayed everywhere.

A hot sun shone on the joyous occasion, as Maxie McCullagh, accompanied by his young wife, alighted from the 'bus and were greeted by his father and mother, and members of the St. Mary's Club reception committee.

Those present included Garda Jim Farren and Messrs. W. A. Power and B. Corcoran.

Standing up in an open car which moved slowly through the streets, Maxie waved and smiled to thousands of greetings from people on the side walks.

Address of Welcome

At St. Mary's Hall, Mr. P. J. Shaw, on behalf of the Mullingar Town Commissioners, present him with an illuminated address. Mr. Shaw, after paying glowing tributes to the champion, then read the address of welcome.

Very Rev. J. Kevlin, Chairman of the Mullingar Boys' Club, extended a hearty welcome to the boxer.

When McCullagh rose to speak after further tributes, there was an outburst of applause which lasted for fully five minutes. He said he felt the occasion was one of the proudest moments in his life.

In the Hibernian Cinema on Sunday night Maxie was presented with two bronze statues mounted on marble by Mr. P. Holmes, Manager, on behalf of the Cinema staff.

KEEPING THE WATER RUNNING

In accordance with the recommendation of the Chief Assistant County Engineer, the County Manager has ordered that the contract of Mr. Eugene Gargan for the maintenance of forty-six pumps in the Delvin and Killucan areas be renewed for a further twelve months to 31st March, 1950, at the rate of £2/10 per pump.

Report on boxer Maxie McCullough's return from his European Triumph, 1949

Jack Charlton visits Kilroy's Store in the run-up to the World Cup, 1994.
From left to right: Tony Keegan, Jack Charlton, Betty Sleator, Derry Kilroy.

Mullingar Athletic Soccer Team around 1983.
Back row, left to right: Barry Rogers, Christopher Coyne, Eamonn Healy, John Smith, Ciarán Jordan, Joe Lynam, Eamonn Dunne, Tom Maguire.
Front row: Gerry Murphy, Ciaran Creean, Eddie Tynan, Denis Shiels, Ken McKervey, Kevin Smith, Liam Loughman.

Mullingar and District Liverpool FC Supporters' Club make a presentation to the visiting Lord Major of Liverpool, Cllr Frank Doran.
Back row, from left to right: Brian Kelly, Tom Morton, Tommy Coleman, Ray McMahon, Cllr Frank McIntyre.
Front row: Cllr Frank Doran, Cllr Ann Keena.

Martin Fagan, U17 All-Ireland CBS Cross-Country
Champion.

Mullingar U15 All-Ireland Cross-Country Champions, 1990s.
From left to right: Paul Hickey, Conor Twomey, Mark Christie (Individual
winner), Richard Price, Jason Brien, Ger Feerick.

NEWBROOK RACE COURSE, MULLINGAR

Above: The racecourse in the early 1900s.
Below: Programme for the horse show.

1899.

MULLINGAR HORSE SHOW,

(SHOW ENCLOSURE, MULLINGAR,)

On Tuesday, 25th July, 1899.

Open to All Ireland for Trained Horses in Classes
V., VI., VII., VIII., IX., and X.

CATALOGUE

According to Entries lodged with Secretary.

PROGRAMME.

10 a.m.	...	... Judging commences
2.0 p.m.	...	{ Westmeath Hunt Produce Cup
		{ The Hunters' Cup
2.30 ,,	...	Parade of Prize Horses
3. 0 ,,	...	Jumping Competitions

ADMISSION.

Reserved Stand and Enclosure	...	...	3/6
General Enclosure	...	...	2/-
Do. (after 2 p.m.	...	...	1/-
Transfer Tickets from General Enclosure to Stand.	...	...	2/6

Price—*SIXPENCE.*

MULLINGAR:

PRINTED AT THE "WESTMEATH GUARDIAN" OFFICE.

Above: A race at Newbrook in the 1940s.

Right: 'Quare Times' on his way to victory at Aintree. The jockey was Pat Taaffe.

Grand National Winner 'General Symonds' leads a charity walk in 1972.

Golf Club subscription, 1933.

Women playing at the new golf course in 1936.

The Westmeath Hunt in the 1920s.

Hunt Ball at Levington Park in the 1950s.

Members of Mullingar Yacht Club sailing on Lough Ennell, 1960s.

Mullingar Karting Club

Chairman	Treasurer
Denis F Shaw	Eddie Jordan

On behalf of Mullingar Karting Club, we would like to express our thanks to all drivers and supporters who travelled in some cases up to 200 miles to this, our inaugural meeting.

Officals of the Meeting

Race Steward	Eamonn Kelly
Clerk Of Course	Paddy Dolan
Paddock Marshal	John King
Flag Marshal	Jimmy Hender
First Aid & Ambulance	Civil Defence Unit
Time Keeper	Miss M Galvin

Junior Chamber Mullingar and the Mullingar Karting Club gratefully acknowledge the financial assistance given by all our sponsors, including the Mullingar Steak Festival Committee, without whose generous help this meeting would not have been possible.

Eddie Jordan lived in Mullingar at the start of the 1970s and was a member of the Karting Club.

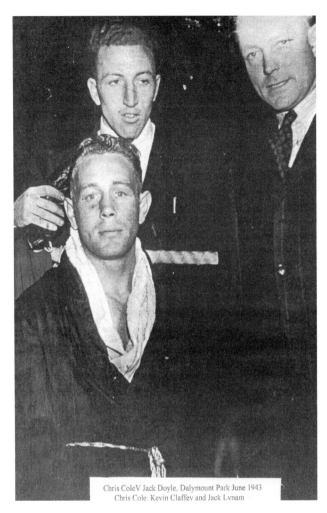

Chris ColeV Jack Doyle, Dalymount Park June 1943
Chris Cole. Kevin Claffev and Jack Lvnam

Left: Boxer Chris Cole at Dalymount Park in June 1943, when he defeated Jack Doyle.

Below: Juvenile handball players, 1975.

These six juveniles are members of Mullingar Handball Club and all were successful in winning West-meath Handball titles in 1976. **Left to right**, Frank Kavanagh (under 12 doubles); John Reynolds (under 13 singles and doubles); Patrick Fitzgerald (under 12 doubles); Charlie Kavanagh (under 14 doubles); Michael McNamee (under 12 singles); Robin McCarthy (under 16 singles and doubles and under 18 singles).

St Loman's Pitch and Putt Club Player of the Year Award.

Mullingar Squash team in the early 1980s.
Standing, from left to right: Michael Greene, John McKay, Tom Hunt, Seamus McGowan.
Seated: Dan O'Dowd, Don Bell.

Joe Dolan and Jimmy White in the Greville Arms with members of St Mary's Snooker Club.

Loreto School hockey players in the 1960s.

SWIMMING CLUB IN MIDLANDS

Above: Christmas Day swim at Lough Owel, 1970s.

Right: The opening of Lough Owel Swimming Club in 1948.

six

Business

At the start of the twentieth century, the town centre of Mullingar looked quite similar to today. The streets were much dirtier and there was much less traffic, but many of the buildings are still immediately recognisable. But with a few exceptions, the shops that were trading in the early and middle years of the century are no longer around and business parks and suburban houses stand where, until a few decades ago, there were fields and even ponds. This chapter is a guided tour of the town recalling the usually small, family-owned businesses which existed in Mullingar before the era of shopping malls and multinationals, when one town's high street did not have exactly the same shops and brand names as every other town. These shops and businesses gave employment to and served generations of townspeople and are worth remembering.

The tour starts at the railway station – one of Mullingar's finest institutional buildings and for much of its 160-year history, a significant employer. Up until the 1960s it would have been a very busy place, with scores of employees, including firemen, boilermen, porters, fitters, telegraph office staff trained in the use of Morse Code, and women selling fruit and other refreshments. Decline set in after 1959 when the lines began to be cut – Clara went and then Cavan.

In 1987, the Athlone–Galway connection also ended. Eason's Bookstall and the Telegraph Office on the Galway platform disappeared. And so did the steam trains – save for excursions run by the Railway Preservation Society, who have a workshop at the station. The first diesel trains ran from 1955. Many of the old steam engines and carriages were taken down the Galway line to be broken up at the gantry, which was one of Mullingar station's most distinctive landmarks. In the 1920s Mullingar station was at the forefront of rail technology when the Brentland track layer was there. But sadly, the technology was used to take up track rather than lay it. By the end of the century, Mullingar had become a busy commuter station for Dublin, but it was perhaps no longer the gateway to the town it once had been. It no longer attracted hoards of boys (and girls) along to watch the trains, nor was it the place from where carts and lorries delivered goods around the town. Many famous people passed through Mullingar by train over the century – royalty, politicians, sports stars, literary figures and genuine heroes such as Alcock and Browne, the aviators. It was the place from which organisations such as the confraternities and the Pioneers set out on their annual excursions to the seaside, accompanied by bands. The railway station was the place where all the various strands of Mullingar – political, religious, military, commercial, cultural and sporting, met and it remains one of Mullingar's most important historical buildings.

At the top of the railway yard the Green Bridge spans the Royal Canal and the railway. To the left, is Patrick Street. In the early 1900s, this was a largely residential district, with many houses built by the Town Commission and District Council in the last quarter of the Victorian era. Many of the residents worked in the station or were soldiers or RIC men. This part of Mullingar would change perhaps less than any other part of the town centre, although the Polish, Lithuanian and Muslim food stores which began to appear on the street in the late 1990s were something that would have seemed unimaginable in 1900. One important business in the street in the early twentieth century was Reynolds' Coach Builders. For much of the twentieth century, Patrick Street marked the western edge of Mullingar.

East of the canal and railway line is Dominick Street. The proximity of the railway station meant that the street possessed two hotels in the early 1900s. On the south side of the street, close to the station, was Brophil's Hotel. On the north side was Kelly's Hotel. Further down

CIE Social Club Dance in the 1970s.

the street on the north side was the Mullingar post office. Mullingar has been a post town since at least 1659 and the post office moved to Dominick Street in the 1850s. Like the bank buildings further down the town, the post office was an imposing structure designed to show the prosperity of the town. The building was sadly demolished and rebuilt in 1981.

One of the landmark buildings in Dominick Street for much of the twentieth century was Mullally's Bakery. Sam Galway's shop, also on the north side of Dominick Street became known as the only shop in Ireland where 'a woodbine, a match, and the time, could be purchased for a ha'penny'.

At the start of the century there was a pump at the eastern end of Dominick Street – vital in the era before the town had a piped water supply. Dominick Square was one of the town's most important market places up until the 1970s. Hay and livestock were bought and sold weekly. The market meant that this was a very crowded and also very dirty place. A weekly fish market would be all that remained of this long visiting Mullingar tradition by the 1990s.

Dominick Street was also the site of Mullingar's earliest cinemas. The Coliseum Cinema was there till the 1960s, on a site now occupied by Dolan's Bar, a place of pilgrimage for fans of the singer Joe Dolan. The name of another pub on Dominick Street, The Yukon Bar, is a reminder of the large-scale emigration of Westmeath men to Canada in the fifties and sixties.

On Dominick Square too, stands what was once the National Bank, which became a Bank of Ireland branch in 1972 and a private college at the start of the new millennium. Cosgrove's Pub across the square has long been known as the Halfway House.

East of Dominick Square is Oliver Plunkett Street. This street was known as Greville Street until 1921, in honour of the town's landlord. On the north side of the street there still stands one of the few shops in Mullingar which has been in business since Victorian times; Day's Bazaar was first opened by Charles Day in 1881. In the early years of the century the Christmas advertisements for Day's Bazaar showed an attractive array of toys.

A few doors down from Day's Bazaar was the Central Hotel, in which Mullingar Rugby Club was founded in 1924. Lipton's grocery store was one of the few businesses in Mullingar in the 1900s that could be considered to be a 'brand' name – part of a national chain of stores. Lipton's later moved across the street and remained in business until the eighties.

From the fifties until its closure in the mid-eighties, Woolworths Department Store was

The Galway platform at Mullingar station.

The fine signal box at the station, which remained in use until 2005.

one of Oliver Plunkett Street's main businesses. Just to the east of Woolworths (now the town centre mall), Joseph Feeley (Town Commissioner) ran a newsagent's for many years until the nineties. Feeley's originally stood across the street at the corner of Mount Street.

In 1900, James Tuite retired as north Westmeath's MP. He was not just a politician of distinction but also a distinguished antiquarian and a businessman. He had a jeweller's shop. In 1917, this business became Walsh's Jewellers and remains in existence to this day.

The Ulster Bank on the south side of the street is a particularly fine example of an early-twentieth-century business premises. Across the street from the bank was Winckworth's

Above: A steam train arrives in Mullingar Station to mark the 150th anniversary of the station in 1998.
Below: Advertisement for Stafford's Hotel and Coffin Makers, 1900.

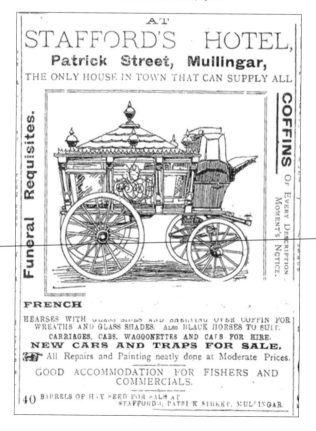

Pharmacy and Gilmore's Hardware Merchant. In 1972, Swarbrigg's Shoe Shop opened in the former Gilmore Shop; the shop was run by a brother of the musicians Tommy and Jimmy Swarbrigg. Andrew Hughes, Butter Merchant, also had a shop on this street. At the beginning of the century, Hutchinson's Drapers was one of the biggest busineses in Mullingar, founded in 1882 by Thomas Lewis Hutchinson from Co. Laois.

Mount Street is now one of Mullingar's most attractive commercial streets. At the start of the century the southern end of the street was dominated by the jail. This building was largely demolished in 1910 to make way for the County Buildings. Beside the County Buildings was the firm of P.J. Weymes, Wool Merchant and Dealer in Hides. Weymes was a Town Commissioner and a major figure in the Nationalist Party until the 1920s. At one point he went bankrupt, but recovered his business. From 1912 until its demolition in 2000, the archway leading to his business premises was one of the landmarks in this part of town.

Another significant figure in Mullingar political life in the early years of the century was Owen Wickham, who served on the District Council and Town Commission and was also a Justice of Peace (JP). He had a grocery business in Mount Street.

Connellan's Bar, located beside the Court House attracted a lot of custom from people travelling through Mullingar on their way north or south. It is possible that James Joyce was among the customers while he was working with his father on the election rolls in the courthouse. The Connellans had come to Mullingar from Sligo and were involved in the Nationalist movement. In December 1903, a reporter described how Connellan's 'Spacious Stores' were filled with 'cases of wines and whiskeys', chests of tea, sacks of flour and meal, boxes of bacon'. The business continued until just before the Second World War.

Later in the century, Larry Caffrey's Bar and Lounge opened, which was one of the town's main musical venues throughout the seventies and eighties. Further up the street, the Midland Hotel also played an important part in the musical history of Mullingar, since Comhaltas Ceoltóirí Éireann was founded there in 1951. At the top of Mount Street, on the west side, was the Arcade or Arcadia – a premises which once housed the Temperance Society, then became a drapery store and, in mid-century a café serving particularly delectable ice cream.

The Market House, one of Mullingar's major buildings has changed little externally over the last century. In 1900, it housed the estate offices of Lord Greville, the Town Landlord. Over the decades, organisation such as the Hibernian Club, the army, the town band and the Town Commissioners used the building, and from 1980 to 1998, it was the venue for a town museum. The square outside was, in the first half of the 1900s, a busy spot, as the weekly market took place there. Another long-lasting Mullingar business stood on the east side of the square; Canton Casey's, Mullingar's oldest surviving pub, was already three quarters of a century old in 1900 and was still in business when the new millennium began.

What is now known as Pearse Street was called Earl Street until about the seventies. On the south side of the street is the Greville Arms Hotel, which in 1900, had just been sold and could proudly boast of having bathrooms! The Greville Arms was the establishment patronised by the gentry and the Westmeath Hunt often met there. It was also the venue, before the First World War, of meetings of the Westmeath Unionist Association. The hotel provided a horse-drawn bus service to bring passengers to and from the railway station. The hotel would remain a rather exclusive venue until the seventies, when it was gradually transformed into a major entertainment venue.

Mullingar post office staff, 1970.

English's Medical Hall, two doors down from the Greville Arms, was run by P.J. English, Town Commissioner and son of Richard English, former master of Mullingar workhouse. From 1912, the Medical Hall was owned by Hugh Weir, and the Weir family were still running a chemist business in Earl/Pearse Street a century later, although at a different address. At the junction with Church Avenue was Gordon's Drapery – an establishment that proudly boasted of supplying tweed jackets to the royal families of Germany and Britain.

On the north side of Earl Street stands the drapery business of J. Shaw and Brothers, which dates back as far as 1875. Further along Earl Street was Joseph Shaw's Grocery Business, which held the Guinness Agency for the midlands. P.W. Shaw Hardware Store was run in the early twentieth century by P.W. Shaw, who served as a Town Commissioner and was TD for Longford Westmeath in the 1920s.

In the mid-twentieth century, Shaw Murray's was one of Mullingar's most popular cafés. In 1972, it moved to Church Avenue where it continued in business for another decade. Other popular businesses along Earl Street included Hughe's Bar and the Oval Bar, whose proprietor was James Bennett, a Town Commissioner and County Councillor in the 1960s and 1970s.

Where McDonalds now stands, there was, in the early 1900s, the much more imposing Nooney's Hardware Store. In 1963, McHugh's Supermarket opened – Mullingar's first self-service store. Two doors down, in 1901, was Phil Shaw's Stationery/Photography. In James Joyce's *Ulysses*, Millie Bloom, the daughter of Leopold Bloom, is working in a photographer's in Mullingar – clearly Shaw's.

Across the road from Shaw's (now Fagan's Office Supplies), is the Lake County Hotel, opened in 1962 by Paddy Fagan, who had made his money in Canada. The Lake County became one of

A cart outside O'Neill's Tobacconists in Dominick Street *c.*1962.

Mullingar's top entertainment venues.

Other businesses in Pearse or Earl Street during the twentieth century which are no longer around included: Parson's Shoe Shop; Porter's Wine Merchant; Kilroy's, which lasted almost a century from 1989 to 2007, the Co-op Store, founded by Michael Clarke in 1920, and the Hibernian Bank (now Bank of Ireland).

Castle Street, north of Pearse Street, has changed much in a century. For more than five decades, the Hibernian Cinema was located there, drawing large crowds to the street nightly. The Presbyterian church and manse dominated the east side of the street and Fenton's Garage was a major feature of the west side, giving off a strong aroma of petrol. To the north-east of Castle Street, on Mill Road, was sited one of the town's largest employers, Flanagan's Saw Mills.

Austin Friars Street, to the east of Pearse Street, was, throughout the century, as it still is, a mix of residential and small business premises.

At the beginning of the 1900s, the most important building on the street was the dispensary, an important part of the welfare system on offer to Mullingar people at the time (Mullingar was one of more than 100 dispensary districts established by the government across Ireland in 1850s). On the south side of the street was Christopher Corcoran's Grocery and Spirit Merchant's premises, Patrick Keena's Shoemakers and Patrick Coyne's Blacksmith's forge. Edward Falkner's Carpentry business was further up the street near the Dublin Bridge. Austin Friars Street in the early 1900s also contained lodging houses, fruiters, plasterers, masons and seamstresses, as well as the home of the Dispensary Relieving Officer.

North-east of Austin Friars Street was Mill Road and the canal. From 1901, the town

Drinkers in Caulfield's Pub in Dominick Street, 1969.

The Fish Market in Dominick Street in 1936.

Dominick Street and Square in the early 1900s. Note the pump and hay cart.

Advertisement for Graham's business, one of Mullingar's
first self-service stores.

Graham's award-winning shop was one of Mullingar's finest food stores. From left to right: Hilda Fitzpatrick, Orla Greene and John Fitzpatrick.

waterworks pumping station was located at the eastern end of Mill Road, beside the canal embankment and tunnel and the River Brosna. Nearby Barrack Steet was a residential area, which, until 1992, included a terrace known as St Andrew's Terrace.

North of Pearse and Oliver Plunkett Street is Bishopgate Street, a largely residential area still, which, at the start of the twentieth century also included the Presentation Convent and its extensive grounds. Until the mid-sixties, the nuns were an enclosed order.

The convent gates and building remain, but the grounds, long the scene of many processions by the Presentation pupils and nuns, are now a housing estate. St Mary's Hall, formerly the lecture hall, was, at the start of the century, a venue for concerts, plays, the meetings of various societies, and also where the Town Commission held its monthly meetings.

In the 1930s, the old cathedral gave way to the new — a dramatic change to the landscape of Mullingar. One consequence of the building of the new cathedral was the demolition of almost an entire terrace of houses – St Mary's Terrace – to make way for a grand entrance to the cathedral grounds.

The biggest change in Mullingar over the course of the century was the massive growth in suburban housing. In 1900, Mullingar's only real residential suburb was the Dublin Road, where doctors, lawyers and other professionals lived in mansions such as 'Belzize', 'Prospect' and 'Bellview'. Where Dalton Park and Ginnell Terrace are now, there was the farm known as Springfield House. From the twenties onwards, however, houses began to be built in all directions. From the fifties, private developments expanded the town still further A whole new Mullingar has appeared just in the last quarter century.

OLIVER PLUNKETT STREET, MULLINGAR.

Oliver Plunkett Street in the 1950s.

The Mullingar Dispensary and Austin Friars Street before 1900.

Lipton's advertisement, 1899.

Staff outside T.L. Hutchinson's drapers in the early 1900s.

Hickey's Butchers Shop in Mount Street in 1910.
From left to right: Joseph Hickey, Mrs Hickey, Paddy Hickey, unknown shop assistant,
Patrick Hickey.

P.J. Weymes's wool business, 1905.

Ladies' Nat. Woven Combinations, short & long sleeves, 4/11

"	"	"	"	6/11
"	"	"	" outsize	7/11
"	Nat. Wool Combinations, short sleeves,			15/11
"	"	"	long "	16/11
"	"	"	" outsize,	18/11
"	Theta	"	short sleeves,	18/11
'	"	"	long "	19/11
"	White Wool	"	short sleeves,	15/11
"	"	"	long "	16/11
"	White Wool Ribbed Vests, short sleeves,			1/11, 2/11, 3/11, 4/6
"	"	"	long sleeves,	2/6, 3/11, 4/11, 6/11
"	Nat. Woven Bodices, long sleeves,			4/6
"	"	" "	outsize,	4/11
"	"	Vests,	long sleeves,	4/11, 5/11, 6/11

We have only a limited quantity of these goods, and they cannot be repeated. The above are in stock.

THE ARCADE, MULLINGAR

Advertisement for 'The Arcade' in 1917.

An invoice from P.J. English's Medical Hall, 1901.

Telegraphic Address—
"ENGLISH," MULLINGAR

27 EARL-STREET,

Mullingar Ap 13th 190 1

Reprs of The Late E. Kilmurry Esq.

To ENGLISH'S MEDICAL HALL Dr.

Physicians' and Surgeons' Prescriptions accurately Compounded.
ANALYSES CAREFULLY CONDUCTED.
ACCOUNTS FURNISHED MONTHLY.

1900			
Oct 8	Mixture	1	8
15	Do Rept	1	8
20	Drops		8
"	Pills		6
30	Mixture	1	6
"	Plasmon		6
Nov 1	Powder		8
3	Mixt Rept	1	6
5	Powd Repts	1	6
7	Mixture		90
"	Powders		6
10	Do Rept		6
14	Powd Rept	1	6
19	Powd Rept		6
	Last Mixt		2
		17	4

WESTMEATH HUNT· RACES·

IMPORTANT!

Please note that **Wm. Gordon** is now making his

FIRST GREAT SHOW

OF LATEST NOVELTIES IN

Boleros, Capes, Mantles, Jackets, Millinery,

DRESS MATERIALS, BLOUSES, ETC., FOR THE SPRING SEASON.
Which have been personally selected from London and other Fashionable Markets.

VISITORS WILL FIND

A LARGE AND EXCEPTIONALLY GOOD ASSORTMENT

IN EVERY DEPARTMENT.

UNSURPASSED FOR BEAUTY, VARIETY AND EXCELLENCE OF VALUE.

WILLIAM GORDON,

COMMERCIAL HOUSE, MULLINGAR.

Advertisement for Gordon's drapery business, 1890s.

Staff outside P.W. Hardware Store. This business is now one of the oldest in Mullingar.

Church Avenue in the 1930s.

McHugh's was Mullingar's first self-service supermarket when it
opened in 1963.

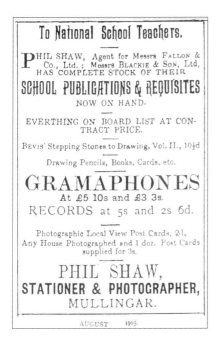

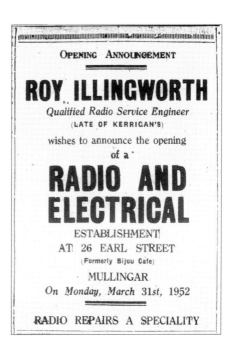

Left: Advertisement for Phil Shaw's, 1901.

Right: Advertisement for a new radio shop, 1952.

Below: Flanagan's Saw Mills was one of the town's largest businesses.

Fine Gael politicians in the Lake County Hotel in 1965.
From left to right: Gerry L'Estrange TD, James Dillon TD, Charlie Fagan, Sean
McEoin, Liam Cosgrave TD.

Jack Lynch, then Taoiseach, in the Lake County Hotel in 1972 with proprietor Paddy Fagan
and local Fianna Fáil councillors Joe Feely and Sean Keegan.

Castle Motors Garage in Castle Street in the 1960s.

Stenson's Key Makers business in the 1980s.

St Mary's Terrace in 1935. Most of the terrace was demolished soon afterwards to make way for the cathedral's main entrance.

Coyne's forge in the 1960s.

The Mullingar Co-op Store in 1920.

Mullingar pumping station.

The demolition of St Andrew's Terrace.

The Presentation Convent and grounds.